the
curiosity
muscle

the curiosity muscle

a story of how four
simple questions
uncover powerful insights
and exponential growth

andy fromm &
diana kander

TrueFolio
PUBLISHING

Published 2018
TrueFolio Publishing
ISBN: 978-0-692-13594-5

Book design by Stacey Aaronson

Printed in the United States of America

the
curiosity
muscle

INTRODUCTION

Toys 'R' Us. Kodak. Research in Motion. Blockbuster. Why is it that companies who capture the imagination of the market eventually lose their touch? How do they lose their relevance with customers?

The scary truth is that **the only thing harder than getting to the top is staying there**.

It may sound counterintuitive, but in many cases, it is the success of a company that eventually leads to its downfall.

Psychologically, success can be dangerous, because it tricks us into thinking of ourselves as experts and it kills our curiosity. Without curiosity about what our customers want, **we develop blind spots about our business**. Blind spots are tension points that our competitors or some eager entrepreneur will be only too happy to exploit.

In fact, that's how *you* reached the top in the first place. You found customer needs neglected by your competitors and swooped in to save the day. Now the question is, can you disrupt your own business before someone else does it for you, and leaves you behind?

Expertise is intoxicating. It makes us feel like we know everything we need to do to make our business successful. We tell ourselves that we know what the customers want, because we know what's worked in the past and we just need to get more efficient with each repetition. But **what worked yesterday may not work tomorrow,** because our customers (and their needs) are changing every day.

As Jeff Bezos brilliantly states:

Customers are always beautifully, wonderfully dissatisfied, even when they report being happy and business is great. Even when they don't yet know it, customers want something better.

What customers went wild for yesterday is the boring, banal, bare minimum they'll accept today, and tomorrow it won't be enough. If you want to stay competitive in today's fast changing economy, if you don't want to become a commodity forced to compete on price alone, you'd better figure out how to consistently find the blind spots in your business and solve them to create new value for your customers.

Feeling like an expert is comforting, which is what makes it such an addictive state of mind. **It's also self-reinforcing**, meaning that the evidence we see as validation of our ideas may actually just be a smokescreen obscuring imminent threats.

Blind spots are not the same as weaknesses, because you can see your weaknesses. In fact, the trouble with blind spots is they can hide in broad daylight, disguised as parts of your business you think are thriving, but have grown woefully inadequate.

Every company moves forward. None of the companies that have peaked and lost their way ever stopped innovating—they never just sat on their laurels. They all continued to introduce new products and services. They all had brilliant marketing efforts. They never stopped making forward progress. The problem was that they were moving the wrong direction—away from their customers and what those customers valued.

The antidote to expertise is curiosity. Curiosity is awareness of the gap between what you currently know about your customers and what you need to know about them.

Curiosity is the understanding that your customers' frustrations with your products or your services is the secret to continuous innovation. Curiosity is the belief that there is always room for improvement. Curiosity is the acceptance that facts about your customers and their view of the world can change overnight and the only way to know when that change happens is to always be asking.

Curiosity is the reason certain businesses don't have to compete on price alone. Curiosity is the competitive advantage the world's innovative companies rely on for continued growth. But curiosity is also a muscle, a reflex—and like any muscle, if it's not exercised, it atrophies.

This book will arm you with the **Four Essential Curiosity Questions** to help you:

- Improve your customer experience in innovative ways;
- Solve persistent problems facing your company; and
- Achieve big hairy audacious goals.

Within these pages is a fictional story that will reveal the Four Essential Curiosity Questions. We've chosen a story instead of a How-To format not because we secretly hope Hollywood turns *The Curiosity Muscle* into a movie (though, look, Dreamworks, if you're reading this, we have thoughts on casting), but because we wanted to create a way to show you rather than tell you what it looks like when curiosity dies within a company—when self-preservation becomes the goal, and customers' changing needs fall by the wayside.

Diana has long been obsessed with curiosity. A serial entrepreneur since the age of fourteen, Diana wrote a *New York Times* Bestselling book called *All In Startup* about what happens when entrepreneurs aren't curious enough about their customers. Her breakthrough business-novel was the tale of a founder who wasted a lot of time and money creating something no one wanted. *All In Startup* detailed conversations entrepreneurs needed to have with their customers in order to test their assumptions and understand if their business idea created any value.

Andy's infatuation with curiosity was always focused on large organizations. He co-founded and built Service Management Group to help large organizations have curious conversations with their customers at scale. At SMG, Andy is responsible for conducting millions of customer surveys every year. *The Curiosity Muscle* presents his experience as an allegory.

This book is the perfect blend of Diana and Andy's approaches, and a resounding promise that companies which prioritize curiosity, and set it at the beating heart of their corporate culture, will create a process of continuous innovation and value creation in their organizations. These curious companies will not only outlast the competition, they will become the disruptors of their industry.

Enjoy the story. Your curiosity muscle is about to get a lot stronger.

CHAPTER ONE

So this was what it felt like to be stabbed in the back, thought John Hunt. To see your life's work wiped out in a matter of days. As he stared down at his fourth beer, John thought about the glass awards, etched with his name, that sat on the shelf in his office—or what used to be his office. They were the accolades he had accumulated at Galati Fitness for growing the company. He imagined they were all in a dumpster now.

Four beers, and he was still no closer to accepting the situation: that after twenty-two years of working his way up the ranks at Galati Fitness, not only was he back at square one, but he had been demoted by his own brother. John looked down at the gold 'GF' logo sewn onto his red polo. Mr. Galati always had a weakness for gold. John felt self-conscious. It wasn't about how he looked in the polo shirt—he was glad that at forty he still had a decent enough body to make it work—but rather about having to wear the polo in the first place.

As the Head of Innovation at the Galati Fitness headquarters, or the Mothership, as Mr. G liked to call it, John could wear what he wanted: sharp-cut suits, workout clothes—the choice was his. After his years working at the gym, he'd grown used to the corporate life and not having a uniform chosen for him.

Now that he'd been sent back to the original Galati Fitness Gym, or GF Zero, as they liked to call it, the gold didn't seem to represent wealth or fame. The letters might as well have been scarlet, he thought.

"Yo, so you used to manage Zero?"

John looked up to see the baby face of his assistant manager, Randy. He, too, wore a red polo. Everybody at Galati gyms did. Randy looked at him expectantly while John tried to formulate an answer. It was John's first day back at the first-ever retail location of Galati Fitness, and it was hard to explain what he was doing there.

"Yeah, I used to manage this place like twenty-two years ago."

"Whoa, bro. That's, like, before I was born. That's nuts!"

That really stung. John took a swig of his beer and decided mid-swallow to just finish it.

"Chug it, dude! That's awesome! You want to do a shot?"

John looked around the hipster bar at all the strange faces. He had thought Randy was just inviting him out alone to get to know his new boss better, but it had turned out to be an entire store outing. Many of the fit twenty-somethings from the gym were there. All were still wearing their red polos. All were younger than him by a decade or more. John wanted to do something to distract from the self-pity and anger. The beers weren't doing much good, so it was time to upgrade to heavier artillery.

"Sure, Randy, let's do a shot."

As Randy made his lithe, youthful way to the bar, John's brain decided that now was the ideal time to replay the conversation with his brother, Roland. It was just like Roland to have done it in his office at the Mothership. A location where he held all the power.

When Mr. Galati, the founder and larger-than-life personality behind Galati Fitness, commissioned the building, he gave the architect only one direction: project strength. Everything, inside and out, was about lifting and feeling powerful. John had always liked that, but he had never expected all that power to be used against him one day. Sitting awkwardly in an office chair that was too small for him, he'd felt helpless as his younger brother explained to him in corporate-speak what was happening.

"Don't look at this as a demotion, John," Roland had said. "It's just that I need you closer to the customers. I need you to get to the field and identify efficiencies."

It sure felt like a demotion.

To make it worse, he had lost a job he had been personally elevated to by Mr. G. He could no longer help bring Galati Fitness back to its glory days—the days to when it *made* fitness trends, instead of just following them. John had been at GF through all the highs, but now that Mr. G had sold the company, those days were long gone. It didn't matter now whom Mr. G favored as his successor, because the buyers had their own savior in mind—and it just happened to be John's younger brother.

A meaty slap on his shoulder brought John back to the present. Randy had shots.

John threw his glass back before he could overthink it. The scorching cinnamon taste made him grimace.

"What *is* that?"

"Goldschläger, bro!" Randy flexed a tremendous bicep. "Breakfast of champions."

It was disgusting. Randy was not showing strong decision-making skills this evening, John thought. Randy had been the one to pick the Pour House, an overly themed bar that felt like a knockoff of a familiar restaurant John couldn't place. Randy was the one who invited everyone else at the gym to join them without checking with John. And now it turned out that he had an affinity for strong alcohol laced with small bits of gold.

John needed another drink to wash the thick burning taste out of his mouth. He walked over to the bar, where a mass of red polos had gathered. They ordered a round of shots (vodka, mercifully) and John felt obliged to follow suit—best to show them he was one of the team.

"Bartender! Una cerveza! And uno mas shot." Oh boy. John only started speaking Spanish when he was tipsy. He had to remind himself not to get tipsy. He was these kids' boss. "Oh! And an agua . . . I mean, a water!"

"Water? Look at you, trying to stay hydrated to keep up with the youth." A woman sat down on the stool next to him. She smiled at the bartender. "Rob, scotch, neat please."

John looked at her, feeling gently wobbly. She was younger than he was. No, wait. Maybe the same age. In yoga pants, casual top, and blonde hair in a ponytail. No Galati polo. She looked at John as if judging him. Not mean-judging him, but a look that made clear that she was expecting a comeback, and it had better not be stupid. John was immediately interested.

"You trying to put some hair on your chest with that scotch?"

Her smile flickered off in disappointment, and she spun her knees in the opposite direction.

Way to go, John. He thought to himself. *Meet a beautiful woman. Start the conversation off with a bang.*

As the bartender set down their drinks, John decided to try again. The alcohol was definitely working now. It was hard to focus.

"Hey, I'm sorry, that came out so dumb. I didn't mean to offend." The woman looked back over her shoulder at him. "I was actually just intimidated by your drink order. How about a toast."

"And what are we toasting?" she arched her eyebrow.

"To intimidating women." John smiled his most charming smile. Something about this woman made him want to keep trying.

"Better," she said, and clinked her tumbler softly against his glass.

"So what's your connection to the group?" John asked.

She laughed. But she still didn't turn her body. Just her face. "I've just belonged to the gym for a while and these trainers are like my therapists."

"Therapists?" The word seemed to stumble on its way out of his mouth. "Anything you want to talk about tonight? I've been told I'm a pretty good listener."

Finally, the woman turned to face him. She looked really familiar, but John couldn't place her. The Goldschläger had gone directly to the base of his skull and was beating it like a snare drum. He tensed up, trying to maintain his composure. *How many drinks have I had? Definitely more than my usual two beers, that's for sure. She's right, I should start hydrating.*

"So, you're new?" she asked. "What's your story? Here to turn this place around?"

"Does it need turning around?"

"Let me guess, you're one of those fancy Harvard MBAs from headquarters."

John guffawed, maybe a little too loudly. This woman thought he had an MBA? From Harvard? "Does reading Harvard Business Review count?"

That earned him a laugh. "Nobody reads that stuff. You just buy it to impress the people on your flight. Plus, you look like you hit the weight bench a lot more than you hit the case studies."

Okay! She likes what she sees. He grinned. "I'll take that as a compliment."

"That's not what I meant." She sipped her whiskey demurely.

"Well, I love all those magazines, HBR, Forbes, Inc. I love learning about what everyone else is doing. I love coming up with the big ideas for Galati Fitness. I've spent my whole life turning this company into what it is." John trailed off. He remembered saying that very line to Roland as he was getting his new marching orders. Why did Roland send him away? Why was his own brother humiliating him like this? He tried to shove the thought from his head.

"So in other words," the woman mused, "you've spent your whole life turning it into a giant bureaucracy that has lost touch with its customers and is on the brink of going out business?"

"Whoa! Whoa!" John held up his hands defensively. "Where did that come from?" He couldn't tell if she was joking or not.

"Too harsh? I'm sorry, that's the alcohol talking."

"That's your first drink!"

She gave it some thought. "So it is."

Who was this woman? She looked like a yoga instructor, but certainly had some business chops. John finished his drink. He thought about ordering another. That was the natural order of things, but he needed to stay on his game now. He reached for his water and gave it one last shot.

"You know, you look really familiar. Have we ever met before?"

"I don't think so," she said.

"Are you sure? Your face just seems like . . ."

"I think I would have remembered."

Is she hitting on me? John wasn't sure how to respond. "I'll take that as a compliment too!"

Another enigmatic smile. "I'll bet you will."

"Let's try names. I'm John Hunt."

"I'm Sam. Nice to meet you."

"You got a last name, Sam?"

She took a deep breath and said it quietly. "It's Donovan."

The name cleared the cobwebs from John's head like a pressure hose. "I'm sorry, *Sam Donovan?* You're the tech queen of the Silicon Prairie?" He paused to make sure he was right. It *was* her. He was sure. "The founder of Sparksys? Oh my God! That's why you looked so familiar! You started the second microchip revolution!"

"Wow, you do actually read those mags." She started getting up from her stool. "It was nice to meet you, John. I'm sure I'll see you around the gym."

"Hang on a sec. Let me get you a drink. You can't just go now."

Just then, Randy walked up with a tray of shots. "You guys want a shot?"

John laughed at the suggestion. He was done for the night. But when he looked at Sam for confirmation, he saw her mouth curl into a smirk.

"I'll tell you what, John." She poked him in the chest with her finger and spoke in that sultry voice. "You get five minutes to ask me anything you want . . ." She picked up the tray of shots from Randy. "For every shot you take."

John didn't know what to say. He had already had more

than enough to drink. He should really be doubling down on the water. Was she even being serious?

"Come on," she waggled the glass at him. "One shot for five minutes. Deal?"

CHAPTER TWO

ROLAND HUNT SHOOK HIS HEAD AND THEN TAPPED HIS INDEX and middle fingers against his thumb—it was his tic when he was annoyed. Not mad—yet—but annoyed.

About fifteen minutes before his operations meeting, Roland had received an interesting email from the finance department—someone had put a massive bar tab on an expense card. When Roland saw the name of the card holder, he'd decided to handle it himself and called Location Zero.

The assistant store manager there said there had been no sighting of John this morning. Roland called John's business cell phone. No answer. Then his personal cell phone. No answer.

He didn't have time for this crap. Literally. Spending time tracking down John meant he was backing up his entire day. There was a meeting with the operations team, followed by a marketing update, followed by several media interviews. He'd barely even begun working on his presentation for the quarterly investors' meeting coming up in a few weeks. The last thing he needed was to be chasing after his brother.

Roland thought about delegating the task down and having someone follow up when they got ahold of John. But that was the problem with family: you couldn't outsource them. He knew that during business hours, he needed to think of John as just another employee, but the truth was that he had always had a blind spot where John was concerned—or at least, he used to. After all, John was older by a couple years and with their mom and dad both working full-time, John had always been there to teach Roland how to do all the basics in life, like frying eggs.

He wasn't sure how old they'd been. John couldn't have been more than eleven, which would mean Roland was seven or eight. The stovetop was a dangerous place at that age, yet John had dragged chairs from the dining room for the both of them to stand on. John showed Roland how to lightly rap the egg against the edge of the pan, then crack it so none of the shell came out. Roland remembered standing there, watching the whites go from clear to opaque as they sizzled in the pan. It was this kind of memory that made Roland try John's cell phone one more time.

Just as Roland was starting to dial, a call came up on his phone. Location Zero. Roland quickly picked up.

"Hey bro!" John's voice was genial. "How's it going? Randy told me somebody was looking for me and when I saw the number I realized it was your office."

"John, did you just get in?"

"Did I just get in?" That was John's tell. Whenever he was stalling for time, he'd just re-ask the question. "Randy just didn't realize I was already here. I was out on the floor with the trainers and I returned your phone call as soon as I saw it."

"How was the morning rush, John?"

"How was the morning rush? It was good. Good good good."

Roland sighed. He wasn't buying it. "Well I'd hope so. I hope it's $900 good. Actually, make that $914.74 good." There was a pause. Roland could hear John muttering under his breath. "John, what the heck happened last night? How do you spend nearly a grand at some bar? Did you buy the place?"

John sounded unapologetic. "Just supporting the local business owners here, Roland. The Pour House is a big community gathering spot. I was building contacts. Hey, you remember that guy who spent fourteen grand at that hotel in Vegas? I don't hold a candle to him."

"Don't try to change the subject, John. What happened?"

There was a long pause before John replied with a sarcastic snarl: "What happened is you sent me here. You told me to improve things. Well, morale needed improving. Mine in particular."

"I'm sure you improved it enormously, John. I'll bet our members are thrilled to have a bunch of hungover trainers assisting them this morning. Let's get one thing clear. I didn't send you there to improve morale, I sent you there to find efficiencies. If we can identify them at one store, we can probably find opportunities to save money nationwide."

"I got it, bro. I'm already on it. I think we should definitely start with single ply toilet paper in the bathrooms. There you go. I think I just saved you like half a mil in annual tissue spending."

Roland took a deep breath. "John, I need you to be a grown-up and take this job seriously. It sounds like you're still upset—"

"Upset? With who? You? *No.* Why would I be upset with you, Roland? Because you demoted me from my own company? The company I told you was for sale? The company whose founder and CEO I *personally promised* that my brother would do a great job. The company I spent twenty-two years of my life building into one of the most respected gyms in the world? Why would I be upset that even though Mr. G named me Director of Innovation before he sold the company, you just—with no notice! No probation!—demoted me to a damn gym manager? I don't know, Roland, would that upset *you?*"

Roland held the phone a foot away from his ear. He knew his brother needed to vent. John hadn't fully grasped what was happening in their initial conversation and he needed to get it out. It was either this or more $1,000 bar tabs. Sometimes that's what a CEO had to do, thought Roland—take the heat. Let people vent, let them get emotional. But it was his job not to get emotional. At the end of the day, a CEO needed to make decisions based on facts and figures rather than emotion.

He let John go on while he silently examined several samples of fitness mats that were on a table next to his desk. He pressed down on each one, testing its springiness, trying to figure out if the price of these new mats was worth it. He gave his favorite one last squeeze and returned to the conversation, cutting off John.

"John, look, it just wasn't working. You tried a number of innovation projects, the employee suggestion contest, the loyalty app, the body scanner . . . we even spent a fortune on delivering home fitness classes. None of these ideas were bringing in the ROI. They weren't making us any money."

"It's only been three years, Roland! This kind of stuff takes time. It takes investment."

"We made investments, John! None of them worked! I'm sorry, but I don't think you're going to come up with the next big idea. Technology is putting new stresses on our business in a major way. We're in a mature industry and there's more pressure than ever on me to figure out how to grow revenues."

"You don't need to tell me about *our* business, Roland. I built this business. I've forgotten more about this business than you've learned in the three years you've been at GF."

"I think I do need to tell you, John. Because you're acting like I think innovation isn't important. It is. That's why I had to take it out of your hands. You simply weren't moving nearly fast enough." Roland's voice had started to rise. He was getting angry. He blew a deep breath out—his therapist had told him to imagine fogging up a mirror. "What I'm trying to say is this. We are facing tremendous competition today, the likes of which you and Mr. G never saw. You two knew a lot about building gyms, but you didn't know how to fight off competition. When this gym was starting off, there weren't many weight lifting places. It was just starting out. Now, we have to compete not just with gyms, but with Crossfit, Orange Theory, boot-camp workouts, not to mention Peloton and other interactive equipment, apps of all kinds . . ." He trailed off. "I have to think about the *future* of this business, John. And the future isn't in some loyalty app."

He waited for John to fire back, but there was heavy silence on the other end. He'd *tried* to say all this when he had John in his office, but he'd gone and stormed out in a rage.

"Our objective right now is to cut costs as much as possible. Find the efficiencies where we can and maximize enrollment. We need to keep this ship afloat as we figure out what the future of Galati Fitness looks like. We need to make sure we aren't just leaving money on the table and we need to evolve."

"It doesn't feel like evol—"

"John. Please. This has gone on too long. I'm going to pay this bar tab. I'm making an entire conference room wait because of you. I just ask that you listen for a second because I understand that you think it's going backwards and I understand that we don't see eye to eye. That doesn't make me a bad guy or you unimportant—it just means we have different views on what this company needs to do to prosper. Use the autonomy I'm giving you. Help me find the efficiencies and I'm not going to bother you or harass you or put you under a microscope. Just don't . . . don't be dumb."

"So, you don't want me to send you an invite to the next outing at the Pour House?"

"Funny."

"It was a one-time thing, Roland. You don't have to worry about me. Go to your meeting. I'm going to go back to work."

"I'm not worried, big brother. See ya."

Roland hung up and heaved out another deep breath. That last line had been a lie. He was worried about John. Hadn't he warned John, over and over, that he needed to take a step back from the canvas? To not take every little thing personally? In the past whenever they clashed about Galati Fitness, it was always because John was too emotionally involved. Cared too much.

But this? John spending a bunch of money and not apologizing, and making jokes when Roland tried to give him advice? That wasn't someone caring too much, it was the opposite. John seemed like he had been checking out mentally for months. Had he finally gone over the cliff?

Roland tried to push the idea out of his head. John was still a little raw, and probably a little hung over. Surely, he'd come around. Everything would be fine just as long as he stayed in his lane and helped implement Roland's plan. A plan that involved cutting expenses while also raising revenue through increased membership prices. The metaphor Roland had used before the board was that the company had been out-of-shape when he took it over and he was going to be its new trainer. His job was to make it lean and fast and he was doing his best.

This speech went over well with the board, but privately, Roland was nervous. The revenue numbers had plateaued, and he knew full well that the only thing that kept them from plummeting was finding new and creative ways to goose prices each year. But how long could he keep that up? This was a short-term solution. He wasn't quite ready to admit that the gym was a dying model, but the evidence was stacking up.

Roland tapped his index and middle finger against his thumb again. The good thing about being CEO was that nobody would so much as frown about him being late to the operations meeting. They should have already started—because unlike Mr. G, Roland insisted meetings continue forward even if a person was missing. It saved everyone's time. It was efficient. It was what he needed John to be.

Roland grabbed his notepad. As he stood up he shook his head, trying to get John out of his mind. Guilt nagged at him, and guilt wasn't a luxury he could afford. And who knew? John could still turn things around. Maybe once the alcohol and shock wore off, this stint at Zero would help him find his passion for the business again.

Or maybe, Roland thought as he left the office, it would be the opportunity John needed to leave and go do something else. Either way, the future was coming, and Roland had no intention of being left behind.

CHAPTER THREE

SAM STOOD IN FRONT OF THE DOOR MARKED MANAGER AT Galati Fitness. Randy had assured her that John was inside. She really did not want to have this conversation, but she wanted her shoes.

Yes, she could try to replace them, but that would involve flying to Hong Kong, finding the weird side street in Sheung Wan she'd wandered down, locating that little shop again—assuming it still existed—and getting her hands on that exact same color and size of leather ballerina flats. It was doable. Maybe. Probably not.

The alternative was definitely doable, but much more embarrassing. She shook her head—*this is what you get for doing something dumb, Sam*. She couldn't believe she'd reached the point in her life where she felt worse about losing the shoes than going home with a stranger. Guess it was part of growing older. And come on—it was her favorite pair.

Sam pumped herself up. *Just knock on the door. Ask for your shoes and go on your merry way. Don't make this into a big deal.*

She knocked on the door. No answer. She knocked again. No answer. Sam thought about leaving and trying later, but she'd come this far already. Gently, she tried the door. It was unlocked.

At the sound of her entrance, John lifted his large head off the desk and looked around in great confusion. All the signs of a mid-morning nap were there: bleary eyes, a little drool in the corner of his mouth, a red flush across his face from laying on his arm. John wiped the drool with his hand.

"Whoa there, champ," Sam said, all nervousness now completely gone. "You look like you got hit by a truck. How ya feeling?" She was scanning the room, looking for her shoes.

"Never better," John croaked. "I was just looking at some, uh . . . numbers." He pretended to pick though some papers on his desk.

Sam tilted her head back and laughed. "Sure you were, Warren Buffett."

John was still coming to, and managed to contort his mouth into something resembling a smile. His eyes slowly came into focus.

"I'm glad you had a good time last night, too," she said. "Dare I say, the most fun I've had at a hipster bar in a long time."

John laughed a little. Clearly he was still shaking off the cobwebs. This wasn't the time for chit-chat. *Stay on task, Sam.* But before she could even think about how to rephrase and ask for her shoes, John was out of his chair and coming over to shake her hand.

"Sam Donovan." He shook his head in disbelief. "It's still crazy that I got to meet you. Sorry I'm a little off my game, you just caught me at kind of a bad time."

"Sleeping?"

John arranged his face into an expression of perfect innocence. "Sleeping? Me? Never. No, I was just resting my feet before getting back out on the floor to see what's going on in my gym."

"Mind if I tag along?" She was building up the courage to ask for her shoes, waiting for an opening. She couldn't tell what he remembered from the night before. How drunk had she gotten him? And what made the Germans think it was a good idea to make alcohol taste like cinnamon and anger?

John led Sam around the main area of the gym. The studios were all against the back wall, with the cardio equipment to the left side of the building and the weights area to the right. Ten-foot-high mirrors ran the length of the walls, and above them were large posters of muscular arms, chests, and thighs with exhortations like ENJOY THE CHASE and GET SERIOUS. They changed periodically, and Sam didn't understand half of them—apparently, they were famous lifter quotes. When she first joined Galati Fitness, she hadn't thought of weightlifters as exactly quotable people, but the more she kept coming, the more her respect for them had grown.

John kept pacing the gym. Sam wasn't sure whether this was actually work or an attempt to walk off the hangover. Finally, she turned to John.

"So, excuse me if I'm being ignorant here, but what are you doing?"

He popped a piece of gum in his mouth and offered her the pack. "Getting a sense for the place. Seeing how things are going. In the military they call it battlefield circulation, and I like to think of myself as the general of this gym."

Well, he didn't lack confidence, that was for sure. She always got attracted to the self-assured ones. "Okay then, Patton. Normal people call what you're doing right now a walk. What are we trying to accomplish?"

"Just trying to take it all in. See how the gym has changed since I was last here."

"It's been twenty years or so, right? Wild. Does it seem familiar?"

John gave her a funny look. "Did I tell you that last night?"

She nodded. Clearly, he didn't remember spilling his whole life story to her the night before.

"Yeah, it's familiar but really different," John said as he resumed his pacing. "It's just, like, the atmosphere feels different."

Sam decided to test her theory. "Yes! That's what I was saying last night!"

He rubbed his temples and squinted at the floor. For a moment Sam thought he was going to say he needed to go lie back down.

"I'm gonna be honest," John said. "I don't remember a lot from last night. I don't usually drink that much. I don't know what you did to me." He winced and pointed to his head. "It feels like my brain's been replaced with used gym socks or something."

Trying not to picture the image in her head, Sam pressed him. "You were telling me that you were frustrated with this place. That they weren't taking innovation seriously."

"Yeah. I mean, I've been working my tail off to come up with big ideas, and this is the thanks I get. They do all this talking about how important new ideas are, and then boom, they kill the whole innovation department and throw me out too. And now I don't know what I'm supposed to do." John looked at her, his eyes imploring.

"Look, I know we just met but . . ." Sam stopped herself. All she had come here to do this morning was get her shoes back, not go white-knighting it back into yet another distressed business. But before her brain could stop them, the words tumbled out of her mouth: "When you were telling me about it last night, it sounded a lot more like the innovation theater department."

"What?" John froze in his tracks. "What are you talking about?"

"Well," she sighed. This was how it always started. Well, at least she liked this John guy. And her shoes weren't going anywhere in his hotel room, she figured. "You told me about the big contest you had where employees got to submit their new ideas, and the accelerator where people got to work on the best ones, but you also told me how nothing ever came out of that. You told me about investing in a loyalty app and new technology, but you never told me how any of the things the innovation team did made any money for the company. Innovation is about creating new value for customers and for the company. **Innovation theater is going through the motions of creating new stuff without ever impacting the bottom line.**"

John was grinning again but this time she could tell it was fake. "You sound like my brother," he said. "And no offense, but you may be Sam Donovan, but I don't think you know the first thing about the gym business." He stopped, grimaced. "I'm sorry. That was too harsh. I think I'm a little hangry."

Sam laughed. It was a totally normal response to suddenly pushing a man into a corner. What did she expect? If she had any hope of getting those shoes back, she needed to make amends fast.

"Oh, I assure you, you don't want to see me when I'm hangry, either. I should have been clearer. I didn't mean you were doing it all wrong. I'm sorry. I think I just phrased it poorly. Still recovering from last night myself."

"No, no," he said, his tone softening, "I'm an idiot. You're Sam Donovan. You started a microchip company from scratch and grew it to thousands of employees. You were an avid angel investor. And did I read that you once won a bracelet at the World Series of Poker?"

"It wasn't the main event."

"Oh, well in *that* case, forget I even mentioned it." John put his most disarming, humble smile on his big mug. "But really . . . I'd love to hear your diagnosis."

"Again?" The shoes might as well have been walking away from her under their own power.

He hung his head. "Oh, God, we already did this, didn't we? I'm sorry. I just don't remember much after the tray of shots."

"Probably for the best that you don't remember." She gave him a smirk. Less for her to be embarrassed about. "I was just saying that I think this place has a much bigger problem than you realize."

He took a step back so that he could lean up against a shoulder press machine and crossed his arms. "And that is?"

Was she really going to go into this again? Of course she was. "GF has lost its curiosity, John. Like many of the greats, the world changed around you and you didn't respond. You know, GF is just like many of the companies that owned 60% to 80% of market share in their category. The inventors of their category. Kodak. Research in Motion. Blockbuster. Sears. Atari. Radio Shack. They never stopped creating new stuff. **But they stopped creating value for their customers because they lost their ability to really understand what customers wanted.** And that's what's missing here." She paused. "In addition to my shoes." *Smooth, Sam. Outstanding work.*

John stood straight up and uncrossed his arms. He ignored the shoes line. "You think GF has lost its ability to understand what customers want?"

"It happens to the best of us. And it happens because we have a lot of success. It's easy to be curious, to second-guess ourselves when we're first starting out. But when we dominate something for a while, we start believing our own hype. We fall into the trap of becoming experts. We start believing that we know the customers better than they know themselves, that we 'own' them in some way—that they're 'our' customers. We assume that just because they found value in our product before, they will continue to do so for the foreseeable future. And those assumptions are just plain wrong. That's why **it's much harder to stay at the top than it is to get there: because it's so hard to maintain your curiosity in the face of success.**"

John exhaled, walked around a bench press, and draped his burly frame over the bar. The gym was pretty empty and there was plenty of open exercise equipment. "Are we talking about GF or me?"

Oh wow. He was listening. This guy might be a little meatheaded, but it's obvious that he cares. "John, it's probably both. I don't know enough to say for sure, but I've seen this story before. All of those greats, the ones who built their own category, **they never saw the disruption coming because they lost touch with their customers.** They lost touch with reality."

"What do you mean, reality?" asked John.

"That their products and services were unsatisfying in some way. And someone else came along and listened to their customers and happily fixed those tension points for them."

"So, that's it? What happened to those companies is happening to ours?" John spun a bench press weight angrily on its spindle. "Great, Galati Fitness is going to be featured in *Inc.* Magazine, under 'What Really Happened?'"

"It doesn't have to!" She came up to him and put her hand

on his shoulder. It was, she couldn't help thinking, an awful lot of shoulder. "The thing about curiosity is that you can always get it back. It's like a muscle." She patted his huge traps. "If you ignore it, it will atrophy and be useless to you, but if you start working on curiosity, you can always strengthen it, you can always get it back. In fact, I made a ton of money off Dominos stock over the last ten years because they figured out how to get their curiosity back. I bought it at four dollars a share in 2009 and nine years later, it was over $200 per share! Crazy, right? They got their groove back, so to speak." She hip-checked him to punctuate her point.

"Domino's, the pizza company? Is this why we got Domino's last night?"

Sam chuckled. "No, the table next to us got Domino's, and you tried to eat it."

John went white with mortification. "I did not."

"It's okay, you were very polite about it."

"Oh, God . . . okay, let's just leave the rest of it a blank. Go back—how did Domino's innovate pizza?"

That was the question she wanted. "Well, the first thing they did was admit that their pizza tasted lousy."

"Ha! I think I remember that."

"Dominos invented pizza delivery. They were delivery experts and that's where they focused all of their time and attention, but they were losing customers and they couldn't see it. They didn't see the problem until there was a national survey done that ranked pizza in terms of taste, and they were dead last on the list! That's what it took for them to get curious again and start listening to customers. To admit they didn't have it all figured out. Can you imagine that? It's like . . . imagine you go on dozens and dozens of dates, and each time you dress your best, you're charming, you're kind, and yet you keep striking out. So you change your clothes, work out harder, go to nicer restaurants, pick up the check, you come armed with new jokes—and nothing works. And then one day someone tells you the truth: you have terrible breath! So you start brushing your teeth better, you start flossing, and before you know it . . . shazam!"

"Huh. And you think we have bad breath? You think our pizza's lousy?"

Sam really wanted to say something sarcastic. But she controlled herself. She wasn't trying to get a job, she was trying to get her shoes back. She needed to wrap it up and find a better way to ask about them.

"Yes, John. Every company has these **customer truths, or tension points, and you can only afford to ignore them for short windows of time** before they start affecting the bottom line. It's low-hanging fruit—it's *right there* in front of them— and most companies are ignoring it. You know why?"

"Why?"

"Because **curiosity is emotionally risky. Finding these things out is embarrassing**—most people wouldn't volunteer to stand in the front of a room and have people they want to impress point out their faults. But **finding opportunities to improve requires facing the challenging feedback.** It's the best way to innovate and stay relevant to customers."

"So what did Domino's do after they fixed the bad pizza? Were there other truths?"

"John, **customer frustrations and disappointments never end. They always have complaints.** Whatever delighted them yesterday is just an expectation today, and it could very well become something they complain about tomorrow. It's a never-ending list of opportunities to create value! After fixing the taste of their pizza, Dominos found customer tension around the ordering process, and tracking their pizza, and God knows what, and now they focus their time on finding new customer tensions every year and working to solve them. Domino's learned how to stop being experts and think more like beginners about their customer experience and all the frustrations they were causing."

John didn't say anything for a while. His shoulders slumped a little. For all his bulk and muscle, all she could see was a man who looked like he needed a hug. She was tempted to give him one, but Sam was not a hugger. She was a talker. So, she talked.

"This low-hanging fruit of innovation exists in every company. That's why the companies who have figured out how to institutionalize curiosity seem to never stop growing. But it usually takes something scary like losing a lot of customers or stagnant revenues, things like that, for most companies to even start looking for that low-hanging fruit. Because, like I said, even though it's always there and has huge implications, it's impossible to see if you aren't looking for it. And every dollar you make is a reason not to change anything, not to rock the boat."

Randy walked up with a stack of towels. "You doing okay, Boss?" He looked chipper and bouncy, like it was just a normal weekday morning. It was easy to forget that less than twelve hours ago, Sam had seen him at the bar performing his one-man karaoke show, despite the fact that it had not been karaoke night. She was jealous of his youthful ability to bounce back.

"Do I look bad?" John asked.

"Kinda do, Boss. You might wanna lay your head on one of these for a while," he said, nodding at the towels.

"I'm starving. I'm afraid I might eat one," John mock-growled. Then he abruptly looked at Sam, "Wait. Did you come to my office for something? I feel like I interrupted you before."

Ah! Finally! The perfect opening! But with Randy here, she didn't want to talk about last night. He'd tell the entire gym, plus Rob at The Pour House, and Rob knew Ellen, her acupuncturist, who knew . . . well, everyone. No, it was best to bring the shoes up later.

"Nope. All set." Sam smiled a fake smile. "Good to see you again John. I'll be around."

"Uh huh." John just looked at her, like he was adding something up, very slowly. Maybe it was coming back to him. She decided to leave before it did, shoes be damned.

At least for now.

CHAPTER FOUR

NEARLY A WEEK HAD PASSED SINCE THE FIRST CRAZY NIGHT at the Pour House, and John had begun to settle back in at GF Zero. Roland hadn't been hassling him, which should have been a relief, but the problem was that no one else from the Mothership was, either. It was as if no one even noticed he was gone. If Roland was trying to teach John a lesson in humility, it was starting to work, because the longer he was out here amid eerie radio silence, the more inconsequential he felt.

John had even downloaded a job-searching app before deleting it. He'd immediately felt like a married man logging on to a dating app, but then reminded himself that he wasn't actually married to GF and re-downloaded the app. He even combed through his emails for all the headhunters over the years who'd sent him come-ons.

For twenty years, he hadn't been able to imagine a world in which he didn't work for Mr. G, but now that Mr. G was gone, there was no sin in just dipping his toe in the job-searching waters to see which companies needed a senior executive who could bench two hundred and fifty pounds and had no college degree. John knew it wasn't the best pitch, but he'd have time to work on it—plenty of time, in fact, because in addition to his phone being eerily quiet, the gym was eerily quiet too, and there was nothing good about that.

John thought his first day there was an aberration. Maybe the first two days. But no: Zero, the birthplace of a gym empire and an entire philosophy about fitness and strength, was nowhere close to full. While small crowds did come for the rushes, treadmills were always available, and so were open spots in classes. People just weren't coming in like they used to.

What was odd was that since Roland had taken over, the revenue numbers of Galati Fitness corporate had been holding strong. Before being sent to Zero, John had assumed that meant that the gyms were packed. Maybe Zero was just an anomaly. Maybe poor management was to blame here. But it seemed weird.

All the more reason to update his resume, which he hadn't done in years. It was just a precautionary measure of course. John wasn't abandoning Galati—never!—but when a boat begins taking on water, the only sensible thing to do is to put on a life vest. His resume was that life vest. He hoped he could salvage the ship, but . . . just in case.

These things were buzzing through John's mind when he arrived at the gym fresh and early on Friday morning. He was mildly excited too. Fridays weren't usually busy after noon, and he was planning to sneak away later and actually look for an apartment, instead of the weird hotel they'd stuck him in. Once he got properly settled, he could get to work. And there was so much to do! So many ideas he wanted to get down—

The TV just inside the front doors was crooked. Something was wrong. It was a big plasma screen and it was at a weird angle, as if somebody had thrown something at it or shoved it.

That was odd. But no sooner had he digested the TV situation than he heard shouting. Despite his imposing size, John had always shied away from confrontation, so any shouting was unnerving—but when it was six a.m. and he hadn't even had coffee, it was doubly so. When it was in a slight accent that he had always thought of as one part New York, one part Eastern Europe, and one part diesel engine, it could mean only one thing.

Mr. G was in the building.

CHAPTER FIVE

MR. G WAS ENRAGED. FIRST, THEY TREAT HIM LIKE A SECOND-class citizen at the Mothership, and now this! Sure, he wasn't the CEO of Galati Fitness or even an employee anymore, but he was still a big-time shareholder—and for God's sake, he founded this company! The Mothership, the five hundred-plus Galati Fitness locations, the whole guiding philosophy had come straight out of his noggin. And now he couldn't get in without a *visitor's pass*?

It was supposed to be a social visit. All he wanted to do was to swing past the old HQ to shake some hands, flex some muscles, and see how the place was doing. He hadn't even gotten past the front desk. The receptionist and security guard had stopped him when he waltzed in. Nope, they said. He needed to check in. Everyone had to get a visitor pass. Roland's orders.

That's when Mr. G explained, keeping his voice even, and with a very humorless smile on his face, that maybe they should call Roland Hunt directly and tell him Mr. G was here to see him. That name alone should have been enough. But then they actually called! And after some murmuring and whispering into a walkie-talkie, the receptionist explained that Mr. Hunt couldn't see him now. That he needed an appointment. Mr. G's smile disappeared, and his voice got louder. Another security guard showed up from somewhere.

So he went to Plan B and asked for John Hunt. John would understand, he'd clear everything up. But then the receptionist checked his computer and made a quick call. John was at Zero, he told him. That was okay, but when was John expected back? No, the man explained, he worked at Zero now.

Mr. G stormed out. He had lost complete control of what was going on at his own company. That very night he'd gotten on a flight to Location Zero. He wanted to figure out exactly what was going on. And what he'd found was that things had gone to hell all over the place.

"What's your name, kid?" Mr. G barked at the young man who was now trying to get him to calm down.

"Uhm . . . Randy, sir."

"Randy, why is the squat box not right here?"

Randy was about forty years younger and six inches taller than the man in front of him, but his hand shook as he pointed to the squat rack.

"It's over there, sir."

"Don't call me sir. Call me Mr. G. and then tell me why you moved the squat rack over there! The angle of the mirrors is perfect for a squat box right here!" Mr. G pointed to his feet. He had done thousands of squats in that very spot. "It's always been here. I put it here! The mirror right here shows if you're going down to depth! And this mirror shows you if you have butt wink!" Randy winced at that term—did he think it was funny? Butt wink wasn't a joke, it was the technical name for a weak posterior, where the lower back and butt gave out below parallel.

Mr. G thundered on. "I'm trying to understand if there's a better reason to have them over there!" Mr. G took a good look at the squat rack he was pointing to about twenty-five feet away. With his eyes he hadn't noticed what was on it at first.

"What the . . . is that . . . a chair in the middle of the rack?"

"It's not a chair, si—Mr. G. It's called a squat cushion. Makes it easier for beginners."

Beginners? Easy? In his day, those two words wouldn't have been *spoken* in his gym! Mr. G felt a sudden urge to throw a kettlebell—which was also in the wrong place! This wasn't healthy. His doctor had warned him about keeping his temper in check; his heart wasn't what it used to be. But what had happened to the empire he'd built?

"Randy! What happened to the TV?" John shouted as he came in.

Finally, a familiar face. Mr. G rushed up to John and grabbed his stomach. "I happened to the TV! And you are getting flabby, Johnny boy!"

"Mr. G!"

They hugged. It was so good to see John that for a moment the anger was gone.

But it was only for a moment. The anger started rising up again. Mr. G waved his arms around him. "Where is everyone? And why is there a kid's potty in the middle of the squat rack? What the hell are you doing in that shirt?" He looked at John's red GF polo. None of this made any sense.

Instead of answering his questions, John kept looking at him. "Mr. G. what did you do to the TV?"

"The what? Oh, the TV!" Mr. G suddenly remembered what had originally made him so upset. "It was that stupid plank video. It just got me all riled up."

"I'm not sure what you mean, Mr. G." John was hesitant. The hug had been enthusiastic, but the rest of his body language didn't really scream *I'm excited to see you.* This was not the John Mr. G remembered.

Two minutes later, Mr. G was in what seemed to be a broom closet. Sure, there was a MANAGER sign on the door, but it couldn't have been bigger than an airplane lavatory—a far cry from his original office here at Zero, an office which used to fit his own private squat rack. That area, according to John, was now apparently a daycare room. Thinking of his blood pressure, Mr. G had tried to remain calm.

John offered him the only chair, then hovered right behind him, along with that Randy kid. Mr. G went to the GF website, and there was Roland and his overly-big smile. His teeth no doubt freshly whitened, his shirt freshly tightened against his skinny arms. The only thing Mr. G could think was that he looked punchable.

Roland started talking to the camera, teeth twinkling, as inspirational music played behind him: "Hey GF team! As the leader of this dynamic and great family of fit-natics, I always try to push myself and those around me." The camera panned out to reveal Roland surrounded by several people in neon workout clothes, colorful mats arrayed before them. They looked like people who had missed their connection at the airport. Roland was the only one who even looked remotely happy.

Roland was wearing one of GF's most popular shirts, which said "do you even lift bro?" Mr. G knew damn well that Roland did not, in fact, even lift. Clearly he didn't understand irony, either. Great. The guy running his business didn't get irony. Somehow Roland kept getting more punchable.

Roland got down on his mat into the plank position. The other people in the video grimly followed suit. He kept in the position as he talked to the camera, his back perfectly straight. "You no doubt have noticed that your local Galati Fitness is getting better and stronger all the time, and it's a shame that we're all keeping this a secret. I'm here to push you to go out there and help share the Galati story with your friends. And I'm arming you with the tools to do it. Each member can bring in up to five new members who will have no registration fee and will get their first month free. And whoever brings in the most members in the next three months at each Galati location will get a cool $1,000 from me!"

The people in the video around Roland were starting to sag in their plank position. One man's arms were visibly quivering. The final shot was a close up of Roland's face, still grinning as he planked. "Are you up to the challenge?"

The video ended, and a silence invaded the tiny room. Mr. G felt both John and Randy looking at him. They seemed puzzled. Why weren't they furious? What was wrong with them? He thought about shouting. Ranting. Cursing until he ran out of breath. That was his normal behavior. His anger-that-will-eventually-pass routine. But no, this was worse.

"Randy," Mr. G said, as softly as he could, "Please give John and I some privacy." Every nerve in his body was twitching trying to control his emotions—and blood pressure. Randy left immediately. As soon as the door shut, Mr. G turned to John.

"Where are all the members? Where's the morning crowd?" he said, keeping his voice as even as he could.

John shrugged. "I've only been here a week and in terms of crowds, I thought the first couple of days were unusual. They're coming for the rushes but there are still treadmills available, still spots in classes. I'm working on it."

Mr. G closed his eyes. Zero was more than a physical building to him. Over thirty years ago, he'd taken over the lease to this very location, pledging his house as collateral. The goal had been to have a cool place for him and his buddies to lift heavy weights and grunt at the top of their voices without anybody staring. He also wanted to throw parties.

Turned out, the idea was a hit. A club where people who cared about their bodies could find a community, provided they worked hard and partied hard. Moreover, the right people joined. The young, hip people, the influencers, the women—all people who had taken Mr. G for a meathead were now fascinated by his views on life and working out.

He opened a second location, staffed with these influencers. Then a third, and a fourth, and so on. Silent partners came in, flush with money. The business took off, and Mr. G became respected and powerful. And it had all started here. This location. The memories were hazy—there had been a *lot* of partying—but they were all there. He couldn't let them ruin this place, and he couldn't let them wreck the company. And even though he didn't have much say in the operations these days, he still had the vast majority of his net worth in GF stock.

Finally, Mr. G exhaled and opened his eyes. He'd had misgivings about the sale, but Roland's presence had reassured him—next to him, no one had ever been more dedicated to his business than the Hunt brothers. John may have been the more passionate one, but Roland, he believed, had the cold logic he wanted in a CEO. He had given Roland the benefit of the doubt and had been hands off and at least outwardly optimistic since the acquisition.

Up until now.

"Johnny, can't you see it?" Mr. G sighed, slumping in his plastic chair. "They're running my company into the ground."

"Mr. G, I don't like it any more than you do! I fought like hell against it, and look where they sent me!" John swept his arm angrily around his cramped little office. "They just have their own set of priorities and refuse to listen to me. But the problem is that whatever Roland is doing looks to be working. Revenues aren't going down."

"That's not real, John. They are deluding themselves. Look around. It's primetime on a weekday and there's nobody here. This place is a leaky bucket. I can smell it. **They are increasing prices instead of loyalty.**" He jabbed his finger into the taller man's chest. "They're charging more for everything they can and hiding it behind shiny promotions and . . . and . . . freaking treating new members better than existing ones."

"Mr. G., you picked the wrong Hunt brother to make your case to. I told Roland the same thing over and over, and the only thing I got out of it was a demotion and a hangover. You should talk to Roland about this! He'll listen to you!"

Mr. G clenched his jaw. "Talk to Roland, talk to Roland. I've had it with Roland! He doesn't care, John. I went to see him earlier this week and they made me get a badge! A badge! Like I'm a salesman or a lawyer or something! He called me on the phone to chitchat for a couple of minutes after he didn't have 'time in his schedule' to see me. And all I could think about was this." Mr. G pulled a mangled visitor's badge out of his back pocket. "They made me wear a visitor's badge at my own company. It was . . ." he searched for the right word. "It sucked."

"Well, how do you think I feel?" John nodded vehemently. "I can't hardly get him on the phone anymore—and even if I could, what would it accomplish? Roland would just pull some numbers to show he's right and we're wrong. The moment I walked in here, I realized it was the same as being banished to Siberia. And it looks like you've been banished too. So welcome to Siberia, I guess. We get red polo shirts."

Mr. G thought about it. John was right. Roland was the numbers guy. His skill was managing them, massaging them, and making them look good. Still, it just wasn't adding up. He didn't have Roland's MBA—he'd gone to college on a football scholarship, and mostly majored in bench-pressing and toga parties—but nearly thirty years in a cutthroat business had taught Mr. G a few things, and the main one was to trust his gut.

John slumped back against the wall. "I just don't think it's as bad as you do, Mr. G."

Suddenly, an idea hit Mr. G, and for the first time all morning, he felt himself smile. "Ok. There's an easy way to settle this, John Boy. We just have to make one phone call."

John stared at him, not picking up what Mr. G was talking about. They used to be on the same wavelength, but it had been a while—John was a little rusty.

"John, I can prove it to you. I can prove that all these new fees are having a bad effect on the business. All you have to do is call you-know-who."

Suddenly, Mr. G was coming through loud and clear. John's brow immediately creased with anxiety. "That's not funny, Mr. G. I really don't need this today."

"You need it more than you know, John Boy. Look, do it for me. It's the last favor I'll ever ask of you. Just one call. Just call Kelsey."

CHAPTER SIX

AT THE SAME TIME MR. G WAS CONVINCING JOHN TO MAKE a call, Kelsey Huerta was getting the Susan Treatment. Not that this was anything new. The atmosphere at the Mothership had swung solidly from people pushing themselves and each other to make the company better to people trying to save their own jobs. She hated how used to it she'd gotten at this point.

"Kelsey, this is really stellar work. Really." Her boss, Susan Bruni, stood in front of her desk searching for the right words. "I'm just a little nervous we're overwhelming the executive committee with so much 'information,'" she said, adding air quotes, "that they won't have time to really dive into it all. And then, what's the point, you know?"

Each week the dance became more pronounced, which meant that Kelsey's boss was more and more concerned for her own job. Like many of the folks in management, Susan didn't want to be responsible for delivering bad news out of fear that she would be cut along with the other 'unnecessary' expenses.

"It's all about 'actionable data', Kelsey. We need to give them information they can act on." And by actionable, what she meant was information that didn't challenge their thinking too much. She meant data that confirmed they already had the right answer and were on the right path.

Kelsey debated whether she should just cut the crap and ask

45

Susan to tell her which data she wanted to pull from the slides, or whether it was worth putting up a fight about why this was important—if for no other reason than to remind herself that there was any fight left in her at all. Maybe she would dip her toe in the water just a little.

"I couldn't agree more, Susan," Kelsey said, in as soothing a tone as she could, "we have to give them actionable data. But what could be more actionable than the fact that the new marketing promotion is bringing in members who aren't actually sticking around? They come for the first month, and then they stop checking in. They vanish. We're celebrating this new membership bonanza, but the whole thing's a sham!"

"Whoa, whoa, Kelsey," Susan checked hurriedly over her shoulder, and lowered her voice. "Let's not throw language like that around, okay? Look, I feel like we've gone over this before. We're not going to make a lot of friends around here by calling out other departments. The marketing team runs analytics on their own programs and it's not really our job to second guess what they are working on. Plus, we have our own priorities. People are looking to us to deliver on the important metrics for this company."

"But these *are* important metrics! The marketing team doesn't even have access to all the data that we can see. All they can see is signups and then they stop tracking, so they think everything is going amazing."

"Kelsey!" Susan sighed in frustration and massaged her temples. "I just feel like I'm not getting through to you. The head of marketing is here—" she held her hand up high in the air above her head. "And the data insights team, we're here." She held her other hand near her waist. "See the problem?"

"Yes. I see that. But what if we just offered to give them this data, with no comment. What if we didn't even say we suspected something was way off about their big new ad campaign?"

Susan rubbed her chin as she considered this. Finally, she nodded. "Okay, I can do that. Sounds like a good compromise. And you'll remove all those slides from our portion of the presentation?"

Kelsey knew that was all Susan really wanted. That she was trying to make her own life easier. Susan wanted to avoid the week of tense, confrontational meetings that these reports would create. She wanted to save herself from the big justifications of why the numbers were wrong. From the frustration of nothing happening as a result. There wasn't any guarantee that Marketing would even look at the data at all; they didn't want to take the chance on being wrong any more than Susan did. Kelsey understood her all too well.

"Yes. I'll remove them."

"I appreciate that *so* much, Kelsey. I think we have a lot of worthwhile data points to talk about with the team. And now with this stuff out of the way, we can focus on the numbers that the executive team wants to see."

Susan reached across the desk for a high five. It was like she knew that what she was doing wasn't right, but if they high fived, then it meant they were both on the same team. Kelsey wanted to roll her eyes but stopped herself. Finally, she obliged, tapping Susan's expectant palm lightly.

Susan walked out the door, proud of her accomplishment and Kelsey slumped back in her chair, disgusted with what just happened. It was like she wasn't just betraying Galati Fitness, she was betraying the data itself—the data she'd dedicated her life to exploring, listening to, bringing to life. Her job was to *report* the data, not warp it! Kelsey made sure Susan was gone before clicking on her happy place: the website for a Buddhist resort for a ten-day silent retreat. She knew it sounded weird—she wasn't a Buddhist, for one thing—but all the reviews raved about how life-changing and serene it was. It was just what she needed. But oh! Then there was the tab for the all-inclusive Spanish resort where every room contained an ocean view. Plus . . . Spanish men! And then there was the tab for the cruise around Belize . . . God, she needed to take a trip. Didn't matter where, as long as it was somewhere, anywhere but the Mothership.

Despite the interaction, she did like her boss. Sort of. Susan was a GF outsider—brought on as one of Roland's hires, as most people in the upper-middle tier of the management had been. They were known informally as a group of "young adults," after an infamous email Roland had sent to everyone at GF the day after being officially named CEO. Roland said he loved GF's culture and wasn't going to change it, but that he was going to grow the company from being a teenager to a young adult. It was corny, but more ominously, it was clear what "young adult" meant. It meant more supervision in the building. More structure. More bureaucracy.

The new policies had actually been good in a lot of ways. The new headquarters was no longer a bro paradise where the walls were covered in bikini calendars. The new headquarters recognized exercises beyond heavy weights. The new headquarters instituted a promotion system based on evaluations and metrics, rather than whether Mr. G could remember your name and if you happened to go the gym at the same time he did and butter him up. In other words the new headquarters had a lot of positives. But at the same time, being a young adult was never as much fun as being a teenager. How could it be? A teenager had no real responsibilities or cares—a teenager didn't have dependents or stockholders. Adults did. And the new GF definitely had more responsibilities.

It was about a year ago that the burdens had started to outweigh the advantages. Especially with Galati Fitness struggling. And if the executive team needed her Excel sheets to prove that it *was* struggling—if they couldn't see it with their own eyes—then they had some even bigger issues. While Kelsey would have thought the answer would have been to directly face down all of these problems, the "young adults" seemed to want to do the opposite—they wanted to plan and forecast, to look past immediate problems into the future.

Her boss was not alone. It seemed like anytime Kelsey wanted to test a new marketing promotion or test current attrition numbers against old data, no one was interested. The young adults were in self-preservation mode and they would rather not check to see if the money they were spending was actually getting them the results they wanted, for fear that it wasn't. Everyone seemed perfectly happy relying on **vanity metrics** like total number of monthly signups, cost of new customer acquisition, or social media mentions and follows. **These numbers** *felt* **good, but they didn't reflect the actual health of the company**. They gave the fourth floor delightful talking points for the board, but Kelsey knew what the real numbers were showing.

It all seemed . . . wrong. It wasn't just Susan who seemed to not want to know the truth, but all of the young adults. They all seemed more interested in saving their own hides than GF itself.

Kelsey's eyes widened: the Spanish resort was offering a singles' weekend. That wasn't something she would have considered this time last year. But now . . . well, forget her boss! And forget the young adults! All of them! If nobody else cared, why should she? Belize or Spain—hell, she'd worked hard, why not both? She could swing the days off. *Come on Kelsey—just buy the plane ticket. Live on the edge!*

Kelsey was looking through the flight options when her cell phone rang. It was a number she had etched into the back of her brain. Her hand froze mid-click. There was no name associated with the number because she had deleted the contact from her phone. She *thought* she'd deleted him from her life. But no, she still knew John's phone number as surely as she knew her own birthday.

She thought about picking up. Not picking up. Changing her phone number. Giving up phones all together. Pretending to be someone else. Hurling her phone out the window and running out of her office and jumping into a cab to the airport and boarding a plane bound for Spain or Belize or Turkmenistan, didn't matter where, as long as it was far away from here.

And then she picked up the phone. Instead of "hello," she just let the silence breathe.

"Hello? Kelsey are you there?" It had been months since she'd heard John's voice, yet it felt instantly familiar—even comforting.

She didn't answer.

"Kelsey? Are you there?"

She took a deep breath. "Yes. I'm here."

"Hey!" he sounded relieved. "So . . . it's been a minute, right? You doing good?"

Another pause. "Is there something that you needed, John?" She heard herself as robotic. Very formal. Like a teacher whose student has disappointed her.

"I sure do!" he said, with a little too much brightness, she thought. "It's totally work-related. But it might take a moment to explain. Do you have a second?"

Kelsey put her phone down on the table and looked up at the ceiling. Her mind was supercomputing, reeling off a thousand calculations per millisecond. He said work-related. Not personal. Was it a ruse? He sounded nervous. He sounded like he was outside. Why would he call from outside? Maybe his car was stuck. Nope—he wouldn't call her. Assume it *was* a work question. But he didn't work in her department. Or on anything she dealt with. So why call her? What did he want? Who cared? Her thoughts went pinwheeling, whirling around her mind until finally, she realized that she was taking too long. She paused just a little more, because, by God, she was going to enjoy her answer.

"I do not, John."

CHAPTER SEVEN

AT THE OTHER END OF THE LINE, JOHN WAS HOLDING HIS CELL in his right hand and clenching his left hand. He could effortlessly lift hundreds of pounds of steel into the air, but right now the phone in his hand felt so heavy he could hardly hold it. This was like pulling his own teeth out. Did she want him to grovel? Well, he wouldn't. He wanted to tell her to grow up, that sometimes things didn't work out. But he said nothing. Still, she didn't hang up. John let the silence sit for a moment. This felt like a chess match, not a telephone call.

"Okay, well, if you don't have anything else, I've got to go." Kelsey snapped.

"Wait, wait, wait! Kelsey! Mr. G is here."

Without waiting for her answer, John handed the phone to Mr. G. She'd talk to him for sure.

"Voodoo! How the hell are ya?" Voodoo was Mr. G's nickname for Kelsey. He had started calling her that about six months after she began working at the Mothership, when her revenue projections turned out to be uncannily accurate. She had tried to explain the reports to him but finally he had waved her off—he didn't understand everything she had done but whatever it was, it seemed like magic to him. "Like voodoo!"

Kelsey was saying something on the other end of the line.

Mr. G laughed. "Yep, it *was* an amazing trip! No. No, that's just a rumor . . . no, not in Thailand either."

John stood and tried to make sense of what Mr. G was saying and how the conversation was going. It seemed like they were exchanging pleasantries at first but slowly the pleasantries dried up and then Mr. G stopped talking much and Kelsey's voice started rising. Mr. G shot an accusing glare at John.

"Well I'm here with him now," he said, as placatingly as he could, "and we were having a debate that I thought only you could settle . . . uh huh . . . uh huh . . . uh huh."

Kelsey was yelling loud enough John could hear her voice bleeding through the phone, though not what she was saying. Mr. G turned his back to John.

"Look, I totally agree, he's a jerk. Huge jerk! But Voodoo, he's my type of jerk. And I need him. Just like I need you. I'm the one who asked him to call. I'm going to lay it all out for you."

This seemed to get her attention. Mr. G's shoulders relaxed. "I think GF is in trouble and the leadership doesn't have a clue. It may not seem like you're headed straight for an iceberg because you're on the ship, but I can see the ship from a distance now. I got perspective." He began pacing the room animatedly, speaking rapidly and stabbing the air with his finger. "I'm telling you, the whole ship's on a collision course and even though I'm yelling *Iceberg!* at the top of my lungs, they got the band playing and they're drinking champagne and nobody on the ship's listening to me." Mr. G nakedly adored the movie *Titanic*. "Except . . . well, except the jerk who initiated this phone call. Sorta. But I don't know if you've noticed, John's not exactly around to let his opinion be known."

There was a pause. Then Mr. G let out a sudden "Ha!" He

turned to John, "She said she hadn't noticed." He plowed on. "Okay. So, you get the metaphor, right? The iceberg and the ship? Maybe I'm off—maybe you think I'm old and cranky. Don't answer that! But I'm telling you something's wrong. And John thinks so too. And—"

A long pause. John strained to hear—Kelsey's voice had dropped, but clearly she was talking, and talking a lot. Finally, Mr. G beamed.

"I knew you'd be in, Voodoo!" He pumped his fist. "We just need you to tell us what the numbers are showing. Is there anything that should cause the leadership to be concerned? I'm putting you on speaker."

Mr. G placed the phone face-up on the table. This time Kelsey sounded a little bit more friendly, but that could be just because she knew her voice was being broadcast.

"Okay. Hi John. Go to hell. I was just saying that no one seems to be listening to me, either. The attrition rate of members is actually much worse than anyone here thinks. They have been looking at a very specific set of data to review attrition, and that's the *percentage* of members that are leaving. But those numbers are being thrown off by the big marketing efforts trying to get new people to sign up at high rates, which means that percentage looks like it's holding steady. But we're spending money on people who either never intend to keep their membership, or we're driving them away somehow after they sign up."

Mr. G slapped John's shoulder. This was the evidence he was hoping for. Kelsey was off and running now. John could hear the heat in her voice.

"What they aren't talking about is how quickly people are leaving after they sign up and why that number has been growing. Members are leaving faster and faster and no one seems to be concerned. I mean, we're about to set a new record pace."

"What does that mean?" Mr. G asked, his forehead creased with concern.

"Look, it's basic human nature to seek out **vanity metrics, numbers that make you feel good about your efforts and show you what's working, but vanity metrics cause you to miss big underlying problems**. It's like the people on the executive team are blind to these big glaring issues. Or they are choosing to ignore them. But something is definitely making people leave soon after they sign up. And at this pace, within nine months, no amount of fee increases or free giveaways for membership can offset the attrition numbers."

"I'm an old man, Voodoo," said Mr. G, pinching the bridge of his bulbous nose. "Speak my language!"

"Mr. G, if they can't figure out why people are leaving and do something about it fast, Galati Fitness is going to quickly start losing money, and if my projections are correct, I think it's going to be a lot of money."

Mr. G pondered this quietly, as John suddenly had a vision of workmen taking down the big Galati Fitness sign from their gym. There had been close calls before—especially in the very early days. But back then the decisions were in Mr. G's hands. Now, thousands of jobs were at risk, and they had no control. If the sign came down from the gym today, all they could do was watch. John knew Mr. G well enough to know that he was suffering the same vision. Perhaps he was questioning his decision to sell in the first place.

"Hello, Mr. G?" The speakerphone crackled. "Did I lose you?"

Mr. G shook his head as if pulling back from a trance. "No. I'm here. For now. So what do we need to do? How do we fix it?"

Kelsey considered this. "Well, something is making the new members unsatisfied. Something is making them stop coming. We need to figure out what that could be. I can't just give you an answer."

The silence hung in the air, draining all the oxygen out of the tiny office. It was common to see Mr. G angry or yelling or cursing. But John had never seen him speechless. Helpless.

It felt wrong to John somehow, to see his mentor this vulnerable and afraid, thrown out of the company he'd spent his life building, only to watch as it slowly imploded. He had to do something. He didn't know what it would be, and it was highly unlikely that their efforts would result in anything, but he owed it to Mr. G to try.

CHAPTER EIGHT

"LET'S PRACTICE OUR 4-7-8 BREATH," COOED THE YOGA teacher, her neon pink tights splendid in the light of the studio. "Breathe in for a count of four. Two, three, four. Now hold it for a count of seven, two, three, four . . ."

If John had been able to laugh in that moment, he would have. But he was too exhausted to laugh. Heck, he was too exhausted to breathe. He'd imagined yoga would relax him and be one of those things that got easier over time, like weightlifting or sit-ups. Instead, John was realizing it was the fitness version of chess—the more he learned, the more confused he became.

It had been a long weekend since Mr. G had shown up. Just as quickly as he had appeared, he had vanished. He'd muttered something to John about needing a few days to think about the phone call with Kelsey and booked it out of there. Part of John was secretly hoping he'd take the weekend to reflect and decide that there was nothing much for the two of them to do, and that this would be the end of it. A calm and dignified end to his involvement with a company that didn't seem to want him or Mr. G anymore. It kind of felt like the days of his relationship with Kelsey all over again, when they both knew it was falling apart—or at least he'd thought they'd both known.

He hadn't regretted breaking up with Kelsey—it had been time. But that still didn't mean it had been easy. He'd purposefully given her space while at headquarters. But this was business, and he needed to keep the personal stuff out of it.

Unfortunately, there was one personal item that had showed up out of nowhere.

There were these shoes. They looked expensive He had stumbled on them while finally moving out of his lifeless hotel room and into a slightly less lifeless apartment. The shoes had been under the bed, just far enough under that somebody wouldn't notice them the first pass through, which made him think they could have been from a previous occupier of the room. Yet they were not hidden enough that housecleaning would have missed them when they turned over the room between guests. Nor was there any dust on them or anything to show they'd been there for a while.

Hadn't Sam said something about shoes? He wasn't sure. But that wasn't the kind of thing you mishear, was it? A lot of words sounded like "shoes." He had a feeling that Sam liked him, but he didn't want to bring it up because frankly, she also scared the heck out of him. It was a weird, almost giddy feeling, but there was just something about her intellect and her business savvy that made him self-conscious. No matter how many business books he had read, he'd never naturally "get it" as well as she did. But he knew he needed help now, and she seemed to understand what had gone wrong at Galati, so here he was, twisting himself into a pretzel two rows behind her at Monday morning yoga class, hoping for an excuse to chat her up about it.

John watched Sam at the front of the room. He wasn't an expert, but her form seemed perfect. Smooth. Effortless. He watched her glide from one move to the next as if it was the most natural thing in the world. John tried not to stare but it was hard not to.

His legs trembling, he tried to focus on his breathing. The class was almost over, but he didn't want to make a fool of himself. But after having kept his mind "zen" for nearly an hour, it was that one last stolen glance that finally cost him his balance.

Not a lot. He didn't completely fall on his face. But he did trip and stumble enough to actually bump the leg of the woman next to him. For a moment, a flash of fear went through him that he had just started a human yoga domino chain. But the woman's balance was better than his—and she kept both her posture and her composure. Well . . . most of her composure. She glared at him, but all John could do was mouth "sorry."

Instead of going into another impossible pose and risk losing the small amount of dignity he had left, John decided to sit on his mat, catch his breath, and take in the class around him. They weren't just the yoga-retreat type with lithe bodies and good vibes, they were the older hip grandma-type and the IT guy who eats a little too much bean dip-type. And yet, they all seemed to be enjoying themselves and nearly all of them—even the grandmas—were able to do the bends and twists that had just sent John sprawling.

His moment of reflection was interrupted by a sound outside the yoga room. On the right side of the studio, the wall was glass and looked out over the rest of GF. It wasn't too busy (it rarely was these days) and immediately John could see a shorter, older, burlier man in a tank top thundering his way toward him, fists clenched. Mr. G was headed right for the studio.

The whole class, the teacher had murmured soft encouragements to "be present," but at this instant John wished he were anything but present. Just as Mr. G reached the studio door, the teacher finally called an end to the class, bowing her head with a "Namaste." The class chorused back, "Namaste."

Before John could finish the greeting, Mr. G was standing over him. He looked excited in the way that people who stay up all night are excited, just before they pass out on the carpet.

"I was right!" He put out a hand to hoist John off the ground, then bear-hugged him. "I'm right! I'm right!"

John could tell when Mr. G was a little loopy. He looked a lot loopy right now. The yoga students were staring at them as they rolled their mats and filed out.

"Mr. G, have you slept since the last time I saw you?"

"Of course! I got forty minutes in an airport lounge in Oakland this morning."

"Oakland? What were you doing in Oakland?"

"I had to talk to people! Not hug some spreadsheets. So after our chat with Kelsey I jumped on a plane and started talking to *real* people! Members! In four cities. Nine locations. I went on a listening tour, Johnny!"

John's eyes bugged out. Mr. G was in his late sixties and in just three days he'd managed to go to as many locations as an old-school, drug-fueled rock band on tour.

"You're nuts," John said.

"Yeah, I am. I'm also smart." Mr. G poked John in the chest. "What have I been going on and on about? Being nickeled and dimed. People hate it with the airlines. People hate it with car sales. And they especially hate it with gyms. Look at this!"

Mr. G reached deep into his old, slightly sweaty sweatpants and John instinctively backed away. But Mr. G had a piece of paper—a little damp, but clearly sporting GF's logo. It even used Roland's "preferred" font.

"I got this in Colorado Springs. A trainer at a gym gave it to me. He presented it as GF's 'à la carte' option. À la carte! What a fancy word for making customers pay for what should be included! They're charging for daily locker use. They're charging for the sauna. They're charging to use the basketball court. Charging for a massage section, which would make sense, if they had actual massages, but no—it's a couple of foam rollers roped off from the rest of the gym!"

"Yeah, we have the same system here," said John. "We've updated the pricing since this piece of paper, but you're right. Roland and his team have jacked up revenues by separating out services."

Mr. G was hopping from one foot to the other. "I did the math and guess what, Johnny. If you add up all this crap versus what was free when I left, to get the GF experience would cost you double what it used to. Two times as much in three years! You want numbers and data and math—there you go! You only need two numbers, two and three. Two times is how much the price has gone up by. Three is the number of years. No, wait—I got a third number for you. Zero! That's how many customers GF is going to have left in another three years!"

"You know, zero is a fascinating number." It was Sam's husky voice. She came up to John, put her hand on his shoulder and gave them both a nod. John marveled at how smooth she was. Even though she hadn't been part of the conversation, her body language immediately made it feel like she belonged. Also, John couldn't help but noticing that she didn't look tired at all after an hour of yoga. If anything, she looked more refreshed.

Sam gave John a nod.

"Hi there, Wobbles," she said seductively. Or at least John thought she'd said it seductively. The woman could have read the menu at Chili's and it would have sounded seductive. He tried not to blush like a middle schooler.

"Mr. G, this is Sam Donovan. Sam, this is Mr. Galati. He's the—"

Sam put up her hand to stop John mid-sentence. "Oh my god, you're Mr. G! I'm a big fan. I read your book like fifteen years ago."

"My book?"

"Don't tell me you're one of those famous people who 'write a book' and don't even read it!"

"No, I just didn't think anyone else did! It was just so long ago. I hope it wasn't boring."

"It was anything but! What a story! You are the embodiment of the entrepreneurial dream!" She let out a subtle laugh. "So, what were you saying about zero customers?"

Mr. G was smitten. "We're saying that's where GF is heading if those bonehead bean-counters at headquarters keep going the way they are!"

"I believe that," said Sam, nodding. "As a GF member I think you're spot on. Like I was telling John last week, when I first joined this gym it was like a well-oiled machine. Serious folks who knew what they were doing. And today, it's like there's a constant parade of brand new faces every day who have no idea what they are doing or what they are after. I'm not talking about lifting technique, I mean the basics of gym etiquette. Like wiping down machines when you sweat all over them or not leaving your ten-pound weight plates on the bench press when you're done. I mean, come on!"

Mr. G cackled and elbowed John. "I like her!" Mr. G's voice got lower and smoother, it was the tone he used when flirting or making a sale. "Now. You have to forgive me—John has many good qualities, but proper introductions are not one of them. Who are you again?"

"I'm an entrepreneur like you, Mr. G. I sold a company a few years ago, and unfortunately, I watched this same thing happen to my baby. New management that cared more about getting a short-term return than serving customers long term. The customers noticed, too, and found other companies who cared more about them."

She toweled the one small bead of sweat off her face and continued. "The new management team was just not curious enough about the customers they inherited. They just assumed they were buying the customers when they bought the company. They thought they were really smart. Smart enough to know what people wanted, what they needed, but the thing is, **human beings are delightfully irrational. It's pretty hard to guess what they want or don't want, especially if you never** *ask* **them.**"

"That's right!" Mr. G shouted, startling a woman passing by the studio. "That's what we need to do, Johnny! We should be going around office to office asking people what they're so upset about, just like the listening I've been doing."

Sam's smile tightened. "Well . . . I didn't mean to eavesdrop, but I did hear the word Oakland and flights and got the gist that you've been on a tour, but it didn't sound like you were doing much listening."

"What are you talking about!" Mr. G asked, his face instantly clouding.

"Mr. G, I heard you when you walked in today. And I'm sorry, but I think you've caught the same plague that's going around your corporate headquarters." Sam pressed her hands together in a conciliatory gesture. "You're not listening because you're **addicted to being right.** You didn't fly around to be curious and understand your customers, you flew around hoping to prove what you suspected to be true. It's not your fault, it's primal. **The more successful a person becomes, the more addicted they get to being right.** It's the number one reason companies miss the simple opportunities for innovation, the low-hanging fruit. They have these huge blind spots for what customers really want because they can't bear to be wrong or to fail, so they ignore the data that tells a different story."

"Young lady," Mr. G stepped back and folded his arms. "That's the most ridiculous thing I've ever heard."

From behind them came a polite cough. John turned; the yoga instructor was by the door. She was ready to go but was afraid to interrupt them. John gave her a wave and mouthed that he'd take care of the room. Then, they were alone. Not that Sam and Mr. G noticed.

"I can prove it to you," Sam poked Mr. G in the chest. Just like he'd done to John so many times. She was smiling and being playful but it was clear from Mr. G's expression that he was no longer smitten. **"Did anything in your conversations surprise you?** Like did you find out anything where you thought, wow, I did not know that, it changes my whole perspective on this problem."

"Surprise me? That's ridiculous. I built this gym. Every square inch. I haven't been surprised by anything since I picked up that hitchhiker in the early '90s."

Sam didn't wait for him to finish, "That's funny, Mr. G. But, **if you aren't being surprised by the responses when you ask for feedback, then you aren't being curious.** You aren't really learning anything new about what's going on with your customers. You'll never discover their truths." Again, John felt that intimidation rising—she was so matter-of-fact. Even he had never been able to talk to Mr. G like this. "It's that simple.

Companies die because they aren't curious enough about their customers' changing needs. They aren't curious enough to ever be wrong."

"Look, *miss*." Mr. G always addressed people properly when he was getting really mad. But Sam's smile didn't waver.

"You want a case study?"

"A what?"

"I'll give you my favorite example of a company that wasn't really curious about their customers and only heard what it wanted. You've heard of Blockbuster Video?"

Mr. G threw up his hands. "I don't have time for this nonsense."

"Just humor me for one second. I'm a big business history buff. I've made a lot of money in the market following curious companies and this is my favorite story. Blockbuster video was growing like crazy. At its peak, it had 9,000 stores, 60,000 employees, and a market cap of five billion. That was the late '90s."

Mr. G rolled his eyes, unimpressed. "Uh huh. I know what happened. They didn't innovate or whatever the buzz word is. Look—"

"No, you look!" Sam cut him off, suddenly taking control. "You think you know the Blockbuster story, but the details are fascinating . . . not to mention applicable. One of my favorite details is that in 2000 they had the chance to buy Netflix for $50 Million! Can you believe that? And the management team very confidently told Netflix no. And then they told them to stop asking. Now, do you think the management at Blockbuster was just dumb?"

No one had a good answer. "I mean, it sounds pretty dumb now . . ." John hazarded.

"No! They were really smart, like you, and they talked to a

lot of customers. In fact, their market research showed that their customers just loved the in-store experience. They loved browsing through the shelves, they loved bumping into their neighbors. They, like you, unconsciously set out to prove themselves right, so they found the evidence that they needed to show their customers vastly preferred shopping for videos in a store to the isolating experience of ordering movies by mail. And were they right?"

Sam didn't wait for a response. "Of course they were right. But the problem was that they were right about the wrong things. They didn't go out looking for their blind spots. They didn't go out looking for surprises. And it turned out that they had a huge blind spot. One that was really frustrating their customers and causing a lot of tension."

It had been over a decade since John had set foot in a Blockbuster, but suddenly the one thing he'd hated more than anything came rushing back to him, clear as day. "The late fees!" John blurted out.

"Yes!" she looked at him with something like pride. "Customers hated those late fees so much that their frustration overcame any warm and fuzzy feelings of shopping for videos at the stores. But the late fees were such a key part of Blockbuster's business model that it never occurred to them to question them. **Most people talking to customers only seek to confirm what they already believe**. I think that you're still a pretty long way from understanding why your customers are leaving because you aren't curious enough. You aren't asking enough questions to find the real blind spots. **Price is rarely THE problem. When people complain about prices it just means they don't think they are getting their money's worth**. There's usually much bigger and lower-hanging fruit."

Suddenly, there was a loud buzzing from somewhere in Mr. G's sweats. Those sweats were like a magician's cloak—somehow he had pockets all over them. He reached in to pull out his old flip phone.

"Ahhh! I told Kelsey to call me this morning! I bet it's her. Kelsey! Perfect timing." Mr. G covered the receiver and turned his attention back to Sam. "We've got to go. It was great to meet you." He flashed her a fake smile. "Appreciate all of your thoughts. We'll definitely make use of them. But we got a company to save."

Sam shrugged. "Good luck saving your company!" She waved to Mr. G and gave John a meaningful look.

Mr. G grabbed a hold of John and led him away. As they made for the office, John trailing in Mr. G's impetuous wake, John had the sneaking suspicion he was forgetting something. It wasn't until they were back in the office, and Sam was surely long gone, that he remembered.

"THE SHOES!"

"The what now?"

"These shoes, they're in my apartment. They're Sam's—they're her shoes."

"Well, call her then."

John looked meekly at Mr. G. "I don't have her number."

Mr. G roared with laughter and slapped John on the back. "Oh man! You're not good at this, John!"

"I used to be," he muttered to no one in particular.

CHAPTER NINE

TWO WEEKS LATER JOHN SAT WEDGED BEHIND HIS DESK IN his little office, trying to go over the most recent membership numbers. But even with his reading glasses on, it was as if the numbers were swimming on the page. He was still wrapping his head around it. By "it" he meant this new job, Mr. G, Sam, the shoes (still in his apartment), Kelsey, life . . . everything.

John's phone rattled on the desktop. He held it to see who was calling, and a crackle of anger went down his spine.

"John Hunt," he said tersely.

"J!" Roland's voice was all slick charm. "Don't tell me I woke you up."

"Huh? Roland, it's after six p.m. I'm at work."

A laugh on the other end. John always thought Roland's laugh had been a bit sinister. "I'm kidding, big bro. I just wrapped up a meeting and wanted to give you a call. Sounded like you might be taking a nap."

"I wasn't napping, Roland."

"No. Of course you weren't. You're hard at work. And speaking of, how's Zero doing? I need those ideas for how to trim expenses!"

"I'm working on it, Roland. Got some theories I'm trying out." John wasn't about to tell Roland that he and Mr. G had come up with a way to fix the pricing problem. That instead of trimming expenses, they'd trimmed fees—or rather, eliminated them entirely. They had just stopped charging the extra fees for towels, the sauna, the foam rollers, everything.

Sure, Roland or someone at the Mothership might notice in a few months or so, but John was the store manager and Roland sent him down here to make a difference. And anyway, their mother had always told them, "it's easier to ask for forgiveness than permission." Mr. G insisted this was the only way to demonstrate the damage the à la carte fees were causing to the business, and Kelsey said she could report back in a few weeks on whether their changes were doing anything to reduce the attrition numbers. John was banking on positive results coming back before Roland noticed anything.

"So, listen," Roland said. "As much as I would love to just banter with you, I'm actually calling to see how you're doing."

"Okay," John said neutrally. Was this a set-up?

"So. How are you doing?"

"Who's asking?"

"I'm asking."

"No, I mean is it Roland my brother asking or Roland my boss?"

Roland weighed this. "Hmm . . . I guess a little of both."

He was being evasive. Well, John could be evasive too. "It's going well, Roland. I'll let you know if I need anything."

"That's it? Nothing more to tell me?"

"Just nice and steady here."

There was a pause. "So, nobody hanging around the gym?"

"Roland, if you got something to say, say it or let me go back to work."

"Fair enough. Listen. Our PR person brought up in a meeting that on social media, people have been posting pictures and reports of Mr. G sightings at your location. I know he was here last month spouting off about how I'm ruining GF. I just wanted to make sure that he wasn't hanging around doing the same with you. That you're not drinking his Kool-Aid about how we need to go back to the late eighties when everything was apparently ahh-mazing and the only thing that mattered in life was how much you benched."

"Okay."

Another pause. "Well are you, J?"

"I'm doing what I can to help GF."

"That's what I thought."

John's lips curled into a sneer. He'd always hated being talked to like a child, but coming from his own little brother, it was intolerable. "Well, Roland, for your information, the executive team is not getting the full picture on a lot of things. Whether that's because people are afraid to tell you or you're ignoring the data, I don't know. Yeah, I've been talking with Mr. G. And yeah, I'm doing a little digging myself. Just because you banished me to Siberia doesn't mean I don't still care. A lot of the employees care. A lot of members care. And Mr. G still cares. They want to help and I'm willing to listen and maybe, just maybe, if the executive committee wasn't so focused on grabbing every single new customer in the world, and charging them every fee imaginable, they would listen to their existing customers. Are you paying attention to the attrition numbers?"

By the time he'd finished, John was out of his chair and slapping the desk with his palm. But Roland had his speech ready too.

"Listen, J. I know you think being around Mr. G again is exciting. That he's paying attention to you. But listen very closely to what I'm about to say. Stay in your lane. I've given you a big responsibility. We need to find efficiencies in the business. Places to trim the fat. I need to find a way to cut over ten million from this year's budget. The attrition numbers are not your problem. That's not your lane. This is me, your brother talking right now. Not your boss, okay? Your flesh and blood. Because if you don't stick to what I've asked you to do—if you keep listening to Mr. G or getting these fancy ideas that you somehow have cracked the code, then I won't be able to protect you. You want to keep your job? You want to help GF? Find the fat. Be a trainer again, not for a client, but for the whole company. I need that money to invest in the future and I need you to just worry about focusing on what I asked you to do."

"And if I don't?"

"Then you get me. Roland. Not your brother, but your boss. I'll can your ass. Just because we don't have the same vision for GF, doesn't mean I don't have a vision myself. It's just that my vision involves answering to investors and making profits. And yours involves reminiscing about the good ol' days. But the good ol' days are gone and warm fuzzy feelings don't drive ROI. Cold hard numbers do."

"Yeah. Well, maybe you're not looking at the right cold hard numbers. Maybe I am."

Roland laughed mirthlessly. "You always were hard-headed, J. Please be an adult about this. This is the last time I'm going to talk to you about it."

There was a click. Roland had hung up. Threatened by his own brother. John could taste the bile rising in his mouth. His heart was racing. His muscles pulsed with anger. He wanted to lift up his whole desk and hurl it through the thin sheetrock walls of his office. He considered it—he could do it. Lift the desk, throw it with a crash through the wall, stride through the gaping hole in a cloud of sheetrock dust and fizzling wiring, walk out the front door and never come back. And what good was all this muscle he'd built if he never *used* it?

Fortunately for both John and the office walls, they happened to be surrounded by other things he could lift less destructively.

CHAPTER TEN

AT FIRST SAM WASN'T SURE IT WAS HIM. SHE KNEW THE handful of regulars who worked out at GF on Friday nights, and the guy benching at the far end of the gym, all by himself, was not a regular, but his silhouette was familiar.

Sam approached, intrigued. It was John, but instead of his red GF polo he was wearing a thin Twisted Sister t-shirt that was darkened with sweat. His jaw was set and his head nodding to whatever music was on his headphones. As soon as John saw her, he clambered up off the bench and plucked an ear bud from one ear. She heard some sort of metal music shrieking.

"Is there a yoga class tonight?" he asked.

"It's strength-training day, John. What about you? Didn't know you were a night owl."

"I'm not. It's just lifting. This . . ." John gestured at the bench, which was glossy with sweat. "This is my therapy. My way of thinking. Steel and metal and me. I'll take that over talking things through any day."

"Something bothering you?"

John smiled thinly and shrugged. Whatever was going on, he wasn't in a talking mood about it. She was about to let him be and do her own workout when she remembered the shoes. He'd already sat back down on the bench and put the earbud back in; she motioned him to take it out.

"Hey John. This might sound a little odd, but have you happened upon a pair of shoes?"

This time he popped out both earbuds and smiled for real, showing some of his teeth. For the first time Sam noticed they were really white. "As a matter of fact, I did."

"That's great!" she exclaimed. "So, uh . . . can I have them back?"

"So, they *are* yours! I found them a while back in my hotel room and was wondering how they got there!"

"I gave them to you at the bar," Sam laughed, then added: "For safekeeping."

John's grin edged closer to a leer. "I'm sure you did. Or you know, is there an off-chance you hand-delivered them to my place?"

She blushed. "Perhaps."

He grabbed a towel and wiped his face down. "Ok, but see, I got a problem. On account of this famous businesswoman feeding me a dozen shots of booze, my memory of that night's a little hazy. Care to fill it in for me?"

"What do you want, a diagram? We're both adults."

"Now that you mention it, I'd love a diagram."

"And I'd love my own late-night talk show, but we gotta play the hand we're dealt."

John smile turned into a sly grin. The adrenaline of lifting had given him his courage back. "All right, I'll settle for a demonstration then."

"Ha!" She burst out. She had to admit, he gave good flirt. "So back to my shoes."

"Whoa! Hold on. You're glossing over the good part."

"My shoes are the good part. Sorry, John. You're not my type."

John gave her a look, "As opposed to who? Randy?"

"Yep, Randy. And Mr. G. And bartenders. And oh, yeah, yoga instructors. All right up my alley. Actually, I'll let you in on a secret." She beckoned him to come closer and whispered: "I'm overwhelmingly attracted to people who don't steal my footwear."

"Well . . . I better keep them then. Don't want you falling for me."

"I'll do my best, Lance Romance. Just bring them with you tomorrow and leave them at the front desk, okay? I'll pick them up."

With that, Sam turned and strode away, her negotiation entirely concluded. It had been a double win. She was going to get her shoes back and she'd navigated the minefield of awkwardness around what happened that night. But she hadn't gone ten paces before she heard, "Sam, wait!" She turned around to see John trotting after her.

"Hey, wait up. Last time we all talked with Mr. G, you said something about how pricing is rarely the problem. I can't get it out of my head."

"You listened!"

"But pricing *could* be the problem, right?" The flirtation was gone from his voice now, she could tell. Maybe this was the problem that had been weighing on him when she walked in.

"It's the *perceived* value that people care about, John. They don't care about price as much as whether they feel they're getting their money's worth. If they aren't, it doesn't matter how many freebies you give them, you're not going to win them back without addressing the underlying issues."

"Well, we talked with customers. This is what they said was bothering them."

"Did you talk to customers? Or did you really listen?" She put her hand on his shoulder, then pulled it back, her palm now bright with sweat. "I think you just went out there to confirm the assumptions you and Mr. G came up with. And Mr. G heard what he needed and wham, bam—problem solved! But think back: was there anything in those conversations that really threw you? Or did it feel just a little . . . easy?"

John scratched his chin. He needed to shave. "I guess it did."

"Think of it like this. What if you were lifting weights that were so light you didn't even have to strain? Would that be making you stronger?"

"That's how every weight feels to me!" he laughed.

She rolled her eyes and groaned. "Sure it does, Mr. Universe. But look—getting feedback is just like weight lifting. **If it feels light and easy, then you're doing it wrong**. You're not growing any stronger. You can only get the real feedback, the surprises, the big insights, if you are curious about your customers and don't assume you already know what's wrong. It's hard. **The more familiar you are with something, the easier it is to feel like an expert and think you already know, but that's when you're going to miss the big areas to improve**."

John sat down on a leg-press bench. "I feel like there's another business parable coming on."

"Oh, if you don't want to hear it, I'm not going to waste your time. I came here to work out, not give out free advice." Sam spun and walked towards the freeweights.

"Really? You're going to leave just like that?" He leapt up and ran after her. "I can't help but think your feet would be so much more comfy in this pair of shoes I happen to have."

"You leave my shoes out of this!" Sam growled, but she

stopped walking. She paused as if she was hesitating about how much to reveal. "You know people pay good money for this kind of advice."

"I know. I take it back."

He seemed genuinely interested, so she relented, "So, of all the questions you asked me that night, very few were about my business, Sparksys."

"I'm a fan. I know all about Sparksys. You guys made the microprocessors for a bunch of computers, right?"

"Yeah. Business to business. Point of sale systems to be exact. Though we were constantly doing other cool stuff too. Like the official computer timers for big sporting events."

"Really? That's cool."

Sam nodded somewhat ruefully. "Yeah. So, microprocessors. You'd think it would be a business where you make the product work as well as possible, and cost as little as possible, and people either bought it or they didn't. When I started Sparksys, that's what I really thought. I was an expert in the product and believed that would be enough. But no, I found out that even in the software and hardware fields, you've got to check your expertise and listen to customers."

"I'm listening."

Sam took a deep breath and folded her arms. "There was a period of a couple years—actually, several years—where I learned the painful lesson that in microprocessors **if you try to compete on price, you'll just go broke**."

She sat down at the bench across from him. "I built this big company and one day realized that it had really stopped growing a few years back. We were stuck . . . we'd plateaued, and we were hiding the slowdown in customer growth by increasing prices bit by bit each year. I tried everything I could to reverse the trend, celebrity endorsements, big marketing campaigns, undercutting our competitors to try and put them out of business. I tried everything but actually talking to customers. I mean, I figured I did that already when I first got started, and what was the point now? And just when I thought we were about to go broke, a customer came to me and surprised me."

She tucked her legs up under her, Indian-style, and brushed a lock of hair behind her ear. John was listening intently.

"Foot Locker came to us and told me they didn't want to buy what we offered. They needed something else. They wanted their POS systems to be able to talk to hand-held bar scanners. Like they wanted somebody to scan a shoe in the back of the store and it would automatically show up in the computer at the front as being in stock. It's par for the course now, but at the time, it was a revolutionary technology, and their old system couldn't handle it. They were considering upgrading every store with a new computer to be able to handle it, but they didn't want to. It was so expensive. They wanted me to help them upgrade just the processors. Sure enough, we were able to design processors that fit into their existing systems and worked with the scanners. And we charged more for our processors! This was a big need I had no idea existed and Footlocker was not the only company interested. That's when I understood just how big this discovery was."

"That customers have these secret needs?"

"Yes! **It wasn't about asking them how much they wanted to pay for what we were offering, but finding out what else we could offer to address those tension points, the frustrations they had with their current limitations.**"

John grimaced. "So, you don't think Mr. G got it right?"

"Look. Mr. G thought price was the problem. His interviews proved it. I'm not saying it's *not* a problem, but he went into those conversations with a bias and **biased questions aren't real questions at all.** They are leading. They elicit the answer that the person asking is looking for. They're closed, narrow questions that try to prove your point rather than uncover anything new. Questions like, 'don't you just hate all these extra à la carte fees?' Totally superficial. You need to dig much deeper to understand what's going on. You need to get a lot more curious."

Sam looked at her watch. She'd already talked too much. "As much as I'm enjoying this, I do want to get a physical workout in."

"But this verbal workout is so fun," John cajoled. "Come on. Just finish this thought process. You've already convinced me to bring your right shoe in. Tell me the takeaways you had, and I'll bring in the left one as well. Please."

"Fine. But there better be a bottle of wine with those shoes. If you take nothing else away from this, remember that curiosity is a muscle, you have to be willing to endure some discomfort in order to really build it. It's hard work to maintain that beginner mindset. Once I figured out that there was a treasure trove of opportunities inside those customer frustrations, I created an annual process by which Sparksys re-committed to its customers and learned their tension points, like we were doing it for the first time. See, people change. Their expectations change. Their frustrations change. **Solving one problem usually means you graduate to a new one.** So, we came up with the Four Essential Curiosity Questions that we had to answer every year to uncover unmet customer needs and frustrations."

"There it is! Let's hear them? What are the magic questions?"

"I thought a gym manager's job was to get people to work

out more, not less," she smirked. "Fine. The Four Essential Curiosity Questions. They kind of require some explanation, but here's the high level: One, what are our blind spots? Two, are we prioritizing the right things? Three, what can we test? Four, how can we engage others?"

"This seems like it needs to be a much longer conversation," John said, trying to keep up by counting on his fingers.

"It's not that bad, and number one is the most important. What are you missing? What tension points are Galati gyms causing for their customers? What's the low-hanging fruit? Remember, **blind spots are not weaknesses that you already know about, they are things you** *think* **you are doing well that are actually frustrating customers.** These four questions and the curiosity process was the best way I could think of to keep my expertise from hurting our company again. I can tell Mr. G has a bad case of the expert mindset because he uses all the clichés."

"The clichés?"

"Experts say things like '**that's not how we do it,**' or '**I know what my customers want, or 'we've tried that already',** or my personal favorite, 'I've been doing this for thirty years!' Experts talk like this because they assume that what happened in the past is how things are going to work in the future. Their expertise makes them believe they can predict the future! And that's just not always going to be the case."

There was a pregnant pause. John looked like he was struggling to take it all in. Sam kept going. "Your brother really doesn't do any of this stuff? He's not listening to his customers or looking for the low hanging fruit?"

"I don't think so. He's a pretty big expert. He's convinced that the key is slashing expenses. That's what I'm supposed to be doing here." John gestured broadly at the gym in general. At a glance Sam could see there weren't more than twelve people working out in the whole building, and most of the trainers were sitting idle.

"Ah. So big brother is the ultimate expert, the knight in shining armor with his Excalibur of efficiency. Or at least he's going to improve the bottom line for a few years. But that stuff never works as a long-term play. **It just diverts all the resources away from the necessary innovations that can actually** *generate* **revenue for the company long term**. I just don't understand why companies can't seem to have a more balanced portfolio approach. It seems like all or nothing. God, it's so *macho*."

"Little brother."

"Huh?"

"He's my little brother, Sam," John groused. "I'm older than he is."

"Well that certainly adds some Shakespearean drama to the situation," Sam mused. "Also, from what I've overheard from you and Mr. G about your brother, why would GF pick a CEO who doesn't work out?"

"Well he does work out. It's just that he only likes planks. That's his thing."

"Wait, planks like elbows on the ground, butt up in the air planks?" Sam looked mystified. "They're a good ab exercise and all, but is that all he does?"

"The plank is to exercising what the unicycle is to modes of transportation," John muttered. It was a line he'd thrown at Roland before, to little avail. "It's a weird thing to be into. But sometime in college, he found this one thing that he was good at. Honestly, I think he's prouder of how long he can plank than he is of all his degrees and promotions."

"That's his thing?" Sam said, arching a skeptical, finely-plucked eyebrow.

"Roland cares about the fact that he can plank for like eight minutes. It's not the sexiest sport but he says he likes it because it's all mental. I think he likes being the best at it."

"Eight minutes!" Sam scoffed. "I bet I could beat that. You probably could too if you gave it a try."

"I have. Trust me. You can't hold a plank that long."

"I bet I could do three minutes right now."

Now it was John's turn to scoff. "Ha! Now who thinks she's the expert? You've got to build up to it. You could do two minutes. Tops."

She jumped up and gave John a playful punch in the chest. "Please. Even an out of shape person can do two minutes."

"All right. Then do it."

"Here?"

John stood up too. "Right here. You're not all talk, are you?"

Sam looked down at the floor. It was a sea of black foam tiles and who knew what else. "No, but I have standards. You got somewhere in this gym where they keep the floors clean?"

"Fine. Fitness room," said John. Then a sly smile crept across his face. "How about a bet?"

"What are you proposing?"

"How about if you can't do three minutes, you tell me what happened that other night?"

Sam was even a little impressed—look who was negotiating now! "I'll tell you if you can beat me. How's that? You'll have to plank it out of me. Deal?"

"I'll take that deal!"

CHAPTER

ELEVEN

SAM AND JOHN FOUND A GROUP FITNESS STUDIO THAT WASN'T being used. Sam thought it would be a piece of cake. John looked pretty exhausted from the bench press and she had all this energy bottled up from work. Plus, she worked her core a lot in yoga. John might have had muscles, but he had a gut, too. Yeah, she had this.

The fitness room John chose was dark. He fiddled with the lights for a moment and at one point the radio came on, but no lights. Sam was getting impatient. Her adrenaline was flowing from the thought of competition and she wanted to get this planking party started.

"Come on, John!" she clapped. "There's enough light coming in from the gym."

She unfurled two mats with a whiplike snap and placed her phone at the head of her mat. Originally, the two mats had been side by side, but John grabbed his mat and positioned it so that he could see the time on her phone too. It meant the top of his mat was practically touching the top of Sam's mat.

They both got down into position. Faces close enough they could have head-butted each other like stubborn rams. Sam gave John a wicked grin.

"Ready. Set. Plank!"

Up onto their elbows and toes they went, and the contest was on. John's legs stretched out and his back went rigid. His arms locked in a triangle on the ground in front of him. He breathed in deep, held it, and exhaled. Then another breath. And another. He took it one breath at time.

Sam was focused on her breathing. She wasn't looking at the watch. She wasn't looking at John. She closed her eyes, trying to block out his breathing. Pain was a temporary feeling, victory was forever. She was a cloud in the sky. A leaf in the breeze.

"Thirty seconds," John huffed.

"Shh!" Sam hushed him. She didn't want to know her time. Her abs were holding nicely—all those extra chaturangas she'd been doing hadn't been for nothing! She became aware of a tightness in her ankles, so she concentrated on those, breathing down to her straining feet. Then her elbows began to ache, so she shifted slightly. Then shifted again. There was a small wobble in her knees.

"One minute," John said. This time, she didn't correct him. The second thirty seconds had seemed to last four times as long as the first thirty. Still, the strain was doable. Her breathing was controlled. It began to feel as if a small child were sitting on her back. John was breathing heavy. She tried not to focus on his breath. Still, it sounded forced. Shallow. *A cloud, Sam! Be a cloud!*

By the time John announced ninety seconds, her abs began to feel like someone was sliding needles between them. Still she held it. She clenched her jaw involuntarily and breathing became harder. Her abs were asking to stop.

"Two minutes." John's voice was ragged now.

Sam's knees were wobbling and her shoulders burned. She'd spent so much time focusing on her abs and clouds, that she'd forgotten other body parts. Her arms and triceps flared with pain. She wanted to stop. It was as if the gravity beneath her had been dialed up, pulling her butt earthward. Every second was a fight to push it back up into the air. She lost all control of her breathing, and tried to will her body back into resilience.

Finally, above the roar of blood in her ears she heard a grunt and then a *whump*. Sam opened her eyes. John had fallen. The contest was over. She finally allowed herself to look at the phone. 2:17. Forty-three seconds more to get to three minutes. Forty seconds. *You can do anything for forty seconds.*

Sweat beaded in fat drops under her hairline and ran warm down her face as she poured the very last of her strength into keeping her butt up.

"Your middle looks like a dolphin," John huffed to her, lying flat on his stomach.

"I . . . (grunt) . . . got . . . (grunt) . . . this . . . (grunt)" she hissed in reply.

She did not. It wasn't a choice. At 2:40. her brain fired an urgent, all-caps message to her butt to HOLD ON FOR GOD'S SAKE HOLD ON, and her butt essentially replied *Sorry new number who is this?* and Sam crashed down to the pink mat.

John looked at her phone. "2:39."

"It was 2:40!"

"Still not three minutes."

They both laid on the mats, gasping for air. Sam wiped her damp brow. Little droplets of sweat had beaded on her eyebrows and the bridge of her nose. She usually only got like this after running for half an hour. John lay beside her, his chest rising and falling like a blacksmith's bellows. She could feel the heat radiating off his face. Neither said a word.

And that's when John made his move. Turned his head and closed his eyes. No hesitation or guile. Smooth as silk, he pressed his lips to hers. Like a prom kiss on the dance floor. Sam was so startled she didn't even have time to think about whether or not to reciprocate.

The lights in the fitness room flicked on.

What? Who? What? Sam whirled on John, who had bolted back from her as if tasered. Her eyes struggled to adjust to the light.

There was a female voice. Then John's voice, choked with horror.

"Kelsey?"

CHAPTER TWELVE

IT TOOK A SECOND FOR KELSEY'S EYES TO ADJUST TO THE
dazzling light in the room, but a second was all she needed to
be flooded with rage. She'd been hesitant to come. Hesitant to
see John. Even once she'd gotten on the plane, she'd gone endlessly back and forth with herself. She'd be fine. She'd ignore
him. She'd talk to him. She'd talk to him while ignoring him.
She thought she'd played out every possible scenario in her
head—but none of those scenarios involved finding John making out with another woman. At the gym. On the *floor*.

Mr. G had asked her—begged her!—to come. To join the
"dream team" he was assembling. Before Kelsey knew it, Mr. G
had booked her an airplane ticket, and was telling her how
valuable she'd be. But really, it was the one name Mr. G didn't
mention that drew Kelsey back: John. The moment she'd hung
up the phone with him that day, a scene had fixed itself in her
mind: John seeing her walk into Zero, and his eyes going wide
as all his feelings for her came back to him in a rush.

She knew it was stupid, but the scene kept playing over and
over in her head, while she was in the shower, while she was
driving, while she was trying to work. She didn't know what
would came after that scene, but at least she'd be the one in

control this time. During the breakup she felt helpless, like a bystander to her own heartbreak. That had been the worst part—she hadn't *done* anything. If she could rectify that while also helping Mr. G, then so much the better.

Plus, what else was she going to do? The fact was that she knew perfectly well that she wouldn't last thirty minutes in a silent Buddhist retreat before she started climbing the walls out of boredom. At least this promised to be *interesting*.

She heard Mr. G enter the room behind her and stifle a snort of surprise. The blonde woman bounded off the mat and came right up to Kelsey. She stuck out her hand. "Kelsey?"

Kelsey wanted to hate her, but the woman's approach was so open and friendly, so genuine, that Kelsey found herself reaching out to shake her hand.

"I'm Sam!" She spoke with such familiarity that for a moment Kelsey thought John *had* mentioned this woman. Her hand was moist with sweat. Kelsey felt like her voice had shriveled up and disappeared. She just stood there feeling ridiculous in the professional yet alluring outfit she'd painstakingly picked out for exactly this moment.

Finally, Sam broke the silence. "Well! I've got to get going! Short workout today. Hi Mr. G!" She turned toward John. "And don't forget. Shoes. Tomorrow."

Before Kelsey could comprehend who or what Sam was, Sam had given Mr. G a hug and left.

And then it was just the three of them—Mr. G, John and her. So this was the dream team. She'd built John up so much in her head over the past couple of weeks that she didn't know what to expect. His face was familiar, but he was sweaty and confused looking. The muscles were all still there but the confidence, the swagger—it seemed to have vanished. He was looking at

Mr. G and then back at her, then at Mr. G and back at her, his mouth gawping but no words coming out.

Finally, Kelsey shrugged her shoulders and said quietly, "Surprise!"

"Did . . . did Roland send you?"

Mr. G piped up. "Headquarters doesn't know she's here."

"Aren't they gonna notice you're gone?" John asked.

So, this was how they were going to do this? Just pretend nothing happened? Fine. She could play that. She shook her head. "I've been saving up my vacation days. I was *going* to go someplace exotic." *And far far away from the thought of you*, she added mentally. "But with things being the way they are at headquarters, I just didn't feel like it. Especially when I started hearing the rumors."

She paused to wait for John to ask her what she meant. It took him a second as if he was trying to clear the cobwebs. Finally, he got there. "The rumors?"

"I think the data program is about get shut down."

"What?" John shot up off the mat. There he was, Kelsey thought. "Shut down data?" John shouted. "Roland is crazy, but he's not that crazy."

Kelsey just shook her head. "It's not crazy. In the short term, it makes perfect sense to the execs. They see the analytics program as costing a lot of money and taking a long time to produce results, and really the only results they ask for are basic things that the accounting department can produce. It's an easy place to cut costs."

"Again, with the cutting costs!" John fumed.

"About a month ago," Kelsey said, "people who I didn't recognize started coming by. Asking me questions. Just hanging out. Took me a while to realize they were from the first floor."

"Human resources?"

"No," Kelsey scowled. "Accounting."

Mr. G groaned. "This is the part that gives me a migraine, John Boy."

"They were asking me all kinds of questions so I started asking questions as well. I found out the reason yesterday and got on a plane here. There's some kind of huge project Roland is investing every available dollar into, including all the dollars from data." Kelsey nodded her head at Mr. G. "I told Mr. G because I thought he might still have some sway. At least maybe he could get me in front of Roland to plead my case to save the department. No dice."

John looked bewildered. "That was yesterday, Johnny," said Mr. G, placatingly. "I was going to tell you, but I figured because of . . . well you know . . . you and Kelsey . . ." He waved his hands vaguely.

"Yeah, yeah," John and Kelsey chorused. They knew what he was getting at.

"Well we're all here now!" Mr. G slapped each of them a little too hard on the back. "It's getting late—Kelsey, you should get some rest before tomorrow. It's been a long day, right?"

She wanted to say it had been a long year. The most trying year of her life personally and professionally. Her long-term relationship with John had disintegrated and now her job was similarly disappearing right in front of her eyes. Instead, she just nodded. "You could say that. Thanks for booking me a room at the Marriott, Mr. G."

"Really?" John looked surprised. "That's right by my apartment."

Mr. G smiled wickedly. "Well! In that case, John can give you a ride back. Give you two a chance to catch up."

Kelsey shot eye daggers at Mr. G. She'd gone from dreaming of the Mediterranean Sea and professional success, to the nightmare of clinging desperately to her job, a three-hour bumpy flight in coach, and seeing her ex for the first time in four months only to catch him making out with another woman. She was exhausted. All she wanted was to get in the bathtub and then go to bed. She didn't want to deal with John anymore.

But she also knew enough not to try and fight Mr. G. Whatever. She'd ride in John's car. But she didn't have to make it easy for him.

CHAPTER THIRTEEN

JOHN'S FACE BURNED AS HE DROVE. THERE WAS SO MUCH he wanted to tell Kelsey. They had been best friends for years. Nobody told him that part of the breakup was that he had to say goodbye to his best friend, not just his girlfriend. He'd tried to date almost immediately after they broke up. There were some bad ones—like the woman he'd met online who insisted on broadcasting their entire first date, with video, to her "beautiful followers" on social media. All he wanted to do at the end of the date was to call Kelsey and tell her how awful it was. It felt crazy that he couldn't.

Over those months, especially as he understood that Roland was freezing him out, it felt like every day there was something new that he needed to talk to her about. But now, with her in his car and the Marriot only ten minutes away, he couldn't think of one thing to say. Not one. His mind felt turbulent, his thoughts tumbling around like clothes in a dryer.

"Red light!" Kelsey shrieked. John's eyes went wide, and he stomped on the brake; his Jeep Wrangler screeched to a halt in the middle of the crosswalk.

For the first time, they looked at each other. Kelsey's face was etched with fury. John put up his hands in a gesture of apology. They stared at each other for a long moment, until the light changed.

"Okay so," John finally hazarded, "can I ask you a question?"

She glared at him suspiciously. "Is it about whether I'm seeing someone?"

"No! No! A business question."

"All right."

John cracked the window; the temperature in the car had gone up by a good ten degrees. "How about just a general moratorium on personal questions. At least for a little while."

"Or forever. Forever works, too," Kelsey snapped.

John let that slide as he considered how to phrase his question. Finally, he just settled on the most direct route.

"Our fee reductions," he said. "The ones we implemented a few weeks ago. You see any difference in the numbers?"

"Ehhh." Kelsey stuck out her hand palm down and waggled it.

"Is that a no or a you don't know?"

"A little bit of both. It's just too early to tell. I mean no doubt revenue was down, even compared to same time last year, but it didn't look like there was any pickup in retention."

"So where did you see a difference, then?"

"I didn't. Sorry, John, but the numbers were, to put it mildly, underwhelming. The same number of people seem to be leaving. I know that can't make you feel good."

"It's fine, you don't have to sugarcoat it for me. The price thing is all Mr. G."

"Really?" Kelsey was piqued. "He told me the opposite. That you were hard charging on cost."

John laughed. "Of course he did." There was a pause as they came to another red light, this time with John making a great show of braking early and carefully. As they waited, John turned to her. "Kelsey, I'll be straight. I love Mr. G but he's so focused on the fact that prices are too high right now that I think we might be missing some other big problems. I think we need to question what we know. We need to get a lot more curious. Find out what's really bothering customers about the gym."

"Why don't you tell Mr. G this?"

"You've met the man, right?" John snorted. "You know how he is when he gets attached to an idea."

"Like a puppy with his favorite tennis ball," Kelsey agreed.

"What I want to do is get customers into a room and talk to them—or get them to talk to us. And with you here . . ." he trailed off.

"So what do you need me for?" Kelsey asked. "Focus groups aren't my department, data is. Is this just about having backup against Mr. G?"

"No! I need someone else in the room when we meet with customers. I just think that there's a good chance I might fall into the same expert trap that happened with Mr. G and the à la carte fees. That I'll just wind up trying to justify my own exper- tise and ideas about the business rather than being curious and listening to customers' frustrations. I need another perspective."

"Why John," said Kelsey, her voice thick with sarcasm, "Whatever makes you think you have trouble listening to people's frustrations?"

John sighed; he had that one coming. Everything about her body language—arms folded, slouching, staring straight ahead—said she wanted out of the car. For a second John al- lowed his mind to wander—they'd had some fun times in this Wrangler. He shook the thought out of his head. Those days were gone. Business, not pleasure. He turned back to Kelsey.

"So are you in? I need your help to make sure I'm hearing what they're saying, not just what I want to hear."

No answer. John drove through downtown; outside, light spilled from trendy cocktail lounges and dive bars. Under the streetlights, couples were strolling hand-in-hand down the sidewalk and ducking into the businesses. They were getting close to the Marriott. Finally, Kelsey lifted her chin and spoke.

"The employees."

"Huh?" John took his eyes off the road to look at her.

"If you're really serious about being curious, you should spend time with the employees too. You and Mr. G have asked for all this data on customers. But there's all this untapped data on employees. It's a gold mine."

"That's a bold statement."

Kelsey turned to face John. "You want bold? How about this—my data shows that **our customer experience will never be better than our employee experience**. As I've been tracking customer satisfaction and attrition, they map almost perfectly onto employee satisfaction and engagement numbers. So if we can figure out how to improve employee engagement, I think customers will also become more loyal."

They arrived at the Marriott. "No kidding?" asked John.

Kelsey nodded, the passion rising in her voice for the first time. "Our trainer turnover is higher than it's ever been, and I have a suspicion that's related to the attrition numbers. And how about this—five years ago, over 60% of our members met with a trainer at least once per month. Today that number is less than 10%. It's great that you want to be curious and really learn what's going on, but I think you can't forget our employees; they might be the most important piece of the puzzle." She sighed and rested her head wearily on her hand. "And not a soul on the exec team wants to hear it."

John felt something unclench inside him. She hadn't said yes, but he still knew her. She was in. He unlocked the car doors.

"Well, okay then. But first. Let's start with the customers."

Kelsey glared. "Did you hear a word I just said?"

John didn't have a chance to respond before she got out of his car and slammed the door. He thought he heard her mutter something about Buddhist monks. He drove away, shaking his head in confusion. She never used to slam the door before.

CHAPTER
FOURTEEN

JOHN WAS ANXIOUS. TOO ANXIOUS TO BE AROUND THE FRONT desk. He went back to a Nautilus chest machine and knocked out a couple reps, trying to burn off some of the energy that was roiling and rattling inside him. Then he jogged back to the front desk, where the receptionist shooed him away, for fear he'd freak out the clients. The big customer interview day was finally here. It had taken a little more cajoling from Mr. G, and a generous offer of letting her use his house in Buenos Aires for an indefinite period of time, but Kelsey had agreed to take a few more days of vacation and stick around and help them round up more gym members to talk to.

They were making progress. Going straight to the source. Getting curious and re-committing to their customers. The only outstanding issue was how to get Sam involved. John still didn't have her phone number. Historically, girls had always asked for his.

As promised, he had brought in her shoes to work and left them at the front desk. He'd been hoping to see her to give them to her in person but just in case, he'd slipped his phone number into the right shoe. But no call had come. No text. As the radio silence grew louder, John began to feel a little sick about it—he'd thought he'd been reading the signs right, but clearly he was wrong. A few days later the shoes were gone, but that was it.

It was too late to turn back now, though. He could do the interviews without Sam. Kelsey had been a godsend. A little standoffish still, but a godsend nonetheless. Still, Sam was the expert, or the anti-expert, who could really make sure this worked. Plus, John wanted to show Sam how he'd improved his plank since their contest in the studio.

Bothered by how comprehensively she'd beaten him, John had done some research on planking. The world record was just over eight hours, which seemed completely unnecessary. Physical therapists and trainers pretty much agreed that there were diminishing returns after ten or so minutes. John wasn't to ten minutes, but he was closing in on four minutes and it had been just over two weeks. It made Roland's seven or eight minutes seem attainable. He'd catch that in no time.

Just as John was thinking about his plank form, there was a commotion at the door. Back in GF's golden days, it hadn't been unusual for eight people to come in at once, but now it was an event. Kelsey was with them. This must be the group.

John had been expecting, well . . . a certain young fit type. The kind of customers Mr. G had always tried to appeal to. These people were all different ages and shapes. Just behind them, though, was a fit, stylishly-dressed blonde woman—it was Sam! She waved to Kelsey who gave her an unimpressed look. If Sam saw the look, she ignored it and made a beeline for John.

"Hello stranger."

"How did you . . . wait . . . are you here for the . . . thing?" John was practically giddy. He didn't normally lose his composure, but he really hadn't been expecting to see her. Much too late, he tried to play it cool. "I mean, uh, it's good to see you. I really appreciate you doing this."

"You can't keep me in the dark," Sam said, patting him lightly on the cheek. John felt acutely aware that Kelsey was watching them. Well, let her watch, he thought. "I just texted Randy and asked him what sort of shenanigans you were getting into, and he told me. I don't think he's cut out for intelligence work," she mock-whispered.

"But Sam—I gave you my number. You could have just texted me!"

Sam winked. "Well, where's the fun in that? Anyway, I hope I'm not too late."

"No. You're right on time." It was Kelsey. Her demeanor had completely changed when Sam walked in. She turned to John. "I didn't know other people were coming."

"Kelsey, Sam is an expert at getting feedback from customers."

"I'm sure she is," Kelsey answered icily. "Anyway, the last couple of members just straggled in. You good with doing this in Studio 2?" Kelsey shot a look at Sam. "I think you're both familiar with that studio." Kelsey walked off toward the group of members before either could answer.

John looked apologetically at Sam, who said nothing. He didn't know how much to tell her. Kelsey clearly thought there was something going on between them, but John was now well and truly confused.

Studio 2 had the most soundproofing and no classes scheduled for another two hours. The people filed in, most grabbing a snack or one of the Gatorades John had set out, then sat on the yoga mats that had been spread out on the floor. Some took advantage of the foam rollers to do a bit of stretching.

Kelsey strode out into the middle of the room, put two fingers under her tongue and gave out a loud whistle to capture everyone's attention. She was all business and in control. John had loved Kelsey most when she was in that mode. And the whistling always impressed him.

"Hey everyone! Thank you so much for coming out to . . . whatever this is. It's not a focus group—we're not here to test stuff on you. Think of it as more of a therapy session. As I told you when I called, I got your names from some people who were familiar with GF who knew you used to be involved customers. Some of you I had to beg to come down here." A chuckle rippled through the room. "Others, bless you, agreed right away. But I'm glad we have both types because I want to hear about your experience. Or more exactly, I want this guy to hear about your experience." Kelsey pointed to John, "John here is the general manager of this gym. He's a big sturdy guy, as you can see, so fire away at him! He can take it."

Kelsey retreated to the side of the room and John came to the middle. He gave her a high five on the way out. Her hand was cool and soft as it slapped his. It was their first physical contact in half a year.

The room felt quiet, tense. All these strangers were looking at him. He'd never been the world's greatest public speaker—he'd never had Roland's smooth eloquence, or Mr. G's raw charisma. His eyes fell on Sam, who was sitting lotus pose in the corner, looking expectantly at John. What would Sam do, he asked himself?

He decided to go right at it, both barrels blazing.

"Okay, everyone. I'm going to ask some questions and I want you to be completely honest with me. Show of hands. Do you feel welcome at Galati Fitness?"

"*Welcome*? Can you be more specific?" asked a middle-aged woman with glasses and crimson-dyed hair.

"You know, whatever that means to you. Does everyone feel welcome?"

All hands went up, albeit with some shrugs.

"Great! That's great news!"

"Welcome, yeah sure," said a younger woman in a pink sweat-shirt next to glasses-lady, "but I quit because I didn't feel good about coming. I mean, everyone was nice, but you guys started doing so many renovations and changing things around. Old machines disappeared, and new machines showed up. For a while, it felt like every time I was coming in it was to a new place. And the trainers couldn't keep up. I came before work so I had to be efficient, and I once spent half my morning trying to figure out where they'd moved the hip abductor, which for some reason turned out to be on the other side of the gym than the hip adductor."

"That does sound irritating," John admitted. "Okay. What about staff knowledge? How many people feel like the staff is knowledgeable?" Most of the hands went up. John was pleased—at least his staff was holding strong. "All right, all right. So staff knowledge isn't an issue!"

There was a loud cough in the corner. John ignored it and continued. "Okay! We're making progress here! Now who here feels . . ."

The cough came again. Louder. Theatrically loud. John followed the source of the noise: Sam.

"*So* sorry, John! It's just this cough. I think I need some water. Can you help me find some?"

"Sam, you know where the water founta—"

"John!" she said. "Help me find the water. Please." She wasn't asking.

John shot a nervous look to the group. Kelsey was rolling her eyes. He grinned at everyone. "Excuse us just one sec."

Sam left the room and John followed. The second John had closed the door behind him, out of sight of the group, Sam grabbed him by the shoulders and practically shoved him up against a wall. The nice, flirty face was gone. Sam actually looked pissed. John was pissed too. He had just gotten started, and she was calling him out in front of all these people?

"This better be good," he hissed.

"What the *hell* are you doing?" Sam snapped.

"What? I'm doing what you told me to do!"

Sam rested one hand on his arm, and pinched the bridge of her nose with the other. "I'm sorry . . . I just wasn't expecting *that*."

"What are you talking about?"

"It just . . . nothing about your questions suggests that you really care what they think. It feels like you're just here to check boxes. Like a restaurant manager passing by a table and asking, 'is everything all right?' Honestly, have you ever in your life said 'no' to that question, even if the food was lousy? No, you just nod, and then you never go back. Because 'is everything all right?' isn't a real question, it's service theater. When people feel like you are just trying to get a certain answer out of a conversation, they are going to be nice to you and give you exactly what you want to hear. They are going to *lie*, John."

Sam took another breath to fully relax. The red flush in her face subsided, and her expression softened. **"You're just not asking any curious questions. You're asking leading questions. And you aren't really listening what they are trying to tell you.** There's a big difference between hearing their words and listening to what they are saying and even what they aren't saying.

Hearing them is passive. You have to dig deeper. There's so much more to that woman's answer about moving the equipment. But you just ignored it because it wasn't on your specific agenda."

"Yeah, well, it's harder than it looks." John replied.

"I know, John, I've been where you are. Mind if I take a stab at it?"

"The floor is all yours." John gestured to the door. He didn't mind her taking over because he was confident that she was about to see that execution was a lot tougher than criticism.

They made their way back into the room. This time John went to the corner.

"Okay!" said Sam brightly as she took the center of the room. "Sorry about my cough but let's get back to it. I have a burning question that John is going to let me ask you all. Tell me about a time when something at GF made you feel uncomfortable or just didn't feel right. Kind of like you, ma'am, when the weights were not where they should have been."

"My last trainer!" a slightly overweight man shouted, and the room erupted into laughter.

Sam laughed along. "Ha! Tell me what happened."

Instantly embarrassed, the man retreated and said, "Oh, I was just making a joke."

But Sam pressed him. "No, no. Tell me about your trainer. The good and the bad."

The member looked around self-consciously. "Okay . . . well, I had this trainer that I just loved and then she 'retired' or whatever a few years back. I think they were cutting her pay or changing around compensation. I don't really know. And instead of replacing her with someone knowledgeable, they gave me this new trainer guy who carried around an iPad that recommend exercises and spent more time plugging crap into that stupid screen than seeing if I was doing my form correctly."

"Oh, the iPads!" A great collective groan went up, so suddenly loud and vociferous that John was taken aback.

"I have a bad back," the man continued, emboldened, "and I just don't think my trainer was very mindful of that. He just kept pushing me to do the Galati Fitness recommended workout. Recommended for who? And who was doing the recommending?"

Sam could see John squirming over by the wall. He looked like he had something to say but was doing his best to contain his thoughts. He rubbed his hand over his mouth, like he was trying to physically restrain himself from speaking.

The room started to loosen up. "I remember one time," said a woman with a soothing classical-music-radio voice, "I had just gotten off the treadmill for this half-marathon I was training for and I was spent. Exhausted and trying not to throw up. And my trainer asked me how I enjoyed that. You'd think good moment. But no. When I looked up, he was physically looking away, he was just holding out his iPad. Stuck it in my face. All he wanted was for me to sign up for the GF 60-Day Challenge."

John couldn't help himself any longer. "Well the challenge has helped—"

Sam flicked out a hand to silence him. "John! Let them finish." She pointed to her right ear and mouthed *listen*.

But now the woman had turned and was talking directly to John. "Don't you get it? I joined to get in shape for me! For myself! Not to help the company with some metrics. I felt comfortable when my trainer was helping me towards my goals. *My* goals! Not whatever goals you guys said I should have."

"I belonged to GF for ten years," said a man who looked

like a triathlete. "Ten years! Trainers. Parties. You name it. I had all the swag. I had the personal locker. I would carry around my trainer's cards for him because people would ask me how I'd gotten so fit, and I could whip out his card and say, 'go to Julio at GF.' But then Julio left. And then they started moving around the free weight section to make room for all the new Crossfit and Orange Theory-type workouts. It was like they were trying everything and excelling at nothing at the same time, just copying a bunch of trends."

"You didn't like the new set up?" John was surprised. "It tested well."

John glanced over to Sam only to see her sending back daggers with her eyes.

"I mean, there was nothing *wrong* with it," the man said, "it just didn't have anything to do with what I was trying to accomplish. And instead of having someone who helped me towards my goals, suddenly GF had these gym-wide goals. Like the crazy plank competition."

"Oh no," John muttered, as another mass groan erupted.

"I didn't care about planks. I cared about the Chicago half-marathon I was supposed to run. But nobody wanted to help me achieve my goals. And GF had gotten rid of all its serious runners and its informal running club and so I felt pretty isolated in the new set up."

"Okay. That's definitely a knowledge gap. And more than that—I'm sorry," Sam softly responded.

Why was she apologizing? She didn't work there! John tried to tamp down his rising blood pressure and take in what they were saying. The group was starting to build up momentum, so much so that Sam didn't even have to ask questions.

"So am I!" the man exclaimed. And with that, the dam was

breached; one after another, the members spilled their stories. They told of GF employees trying to sell them workout DVDs while they were mid-rep. They groaned about the endless up-selling. "It was like working out at a used car dealership rather than a gym," said a woman, and the others nodded vigorously.

John tried to listen to exactly what they were saying. What he heard was that their trainers and employees were pushing products and services onto the customers in a way that made them uncomfortable. And that the GF goals were being pushed on members as if they took priority over their personal goals. John began to realize that even the customers hadn't been completely certain of why they were unhappy—even now, sitting on mats, they were working together to figure out how to describe their frustrations. It was very possible that these interactions between the trainers and members could have been impacting attrition numbers.

John also tried to think about what he wasn't hearing in the conversation, like Sam had directed. Only one guy brought up the à la carte pricing or fees. That was a huge shock. And even then, that one guy was much more concerned by how he was being treated like a walking dollar sign by the trainers.

The session was only supposed to go an hour, but it went nearly ninety minutes before John could tell it was losing steam. He took over from Sam, who had barely needed to speak at all for the last half, preferring only to occasionally recall something that had been said earlier, and thanked all the members for their time as they filed out.

Finally, John, Sam, and Kelsey were alone in studio 2. The air in the room was glacial. Kelsey was still in the corner. John could tell from her crossed arms and wide stance that she wasn't feeling warm and fuzzy. She had seemed to warm up to Sam over the session as she saw the value she was bringing–John could see her furiously taking notes—but now that the session was over, she was back to being distant.

Could he blame her, though? The session definitely hadn't gone according to plan. It had been productive, surely, but it had also been . . . well, what was the word? Humiliating.

But he couldn't deny that Sam had gotten great answers out of the members. This, he realized, was what she'd meant about the difference between hearing and listening. He had never thought about the difference between the two. Now it was all he could think about.

Sam looked at John. "How you doing there, champ?"

"Oof," said John, rubbing his right temple. "It might have taken a few years off my life, but I have to hand it to you. You know what it was? It was bittersweet. Bitter because I heard all these stories of the old GF that people fell in love with—that I fell in love with. Sweet because it was kind of inspiring to think that a gym can mean that much."

"You know that feeling of surprise and pain? The feeling like you were getting shivved in the side as each member lobbed their complaints at you?"

"Yes. I definitely got that feeling."

"It was new, right? You haven't felt that before."

John reflected on her question. "Not from members."

"You've got to remember that feeling John. That's what real feedback feels like. **If you aren't surprised or uncomfortable by your customer's responses, then you aren't digging deep enough**."

"Well, we seem to have hit the motherlode. I mean, we must have a list of over a hundred things we could be working on."

Sam looked at him kindly. "Just remember, you can't fix all

of it. Customers are going to tell you all kinds of problems. Your job is to decide *where* to focus. That's **Essential Curiosity Question #2: Are you Focused on the Right Things?** If you tried to fix everything they asked for today, you'd go out of business. You need to find the thread, those points of tension that are feeding the others and having a financial impact on your business. It means pretty much ignoring most of the comments and prioritizing the biggest insights or blind spots."

"You think it's a good idea to ignore most of the customer feedback?" John asked incredulously.

"It's not that you ignore most feedback. You listen carefully and listen for the few tension points that most customers are talking about. You can't afford to do everything really well. So you pick the few things you are going to focus on that are going to drive the most value and you ignore all the one-off ideas that seem to flow endlessly. You just want to figure out what in the data has the strongest relationship to a financial impact."

"That's a good point. And I feel more curious than ever." He gave Sam a big smile. "Is it crazy that I kind of feel, like, amped? Like this is just the beginning. I want to talk to even more people."

Sam pointed at him in warning. "Talk? You mean listen to more people."

"Right! Listen."

CHAPTER
FIFTEEN

JOHN GOT INTO THE WRANGLER AND TURNED IT ON. EXHAUSTED, he was about to go home. But instead, he shut the car off and leaned back in the seat. Something was bothering him, something he couldn't put a name to. He ransacked the cabinets of his brain. It was like his mind was hiding it from him.

And then the answer toppled off a shelf and hit him right between the eyes.

John pulled out his phone and searched for local trainers on a site he knew that listed and rated trainers. The list was long. John fished around the console on the side of his door. It took him a moment, but he finally found a pen and the back of a receipt to write on. As he scrolled down the list of trainers, he found several names that looked familiar. He wrote them all down. It was a start.

This time John started the car with conviction, shifted into drive, and took off. His own brain had been telling him he was missing something and now he knew what it was: while members had great insights, they were only one side of the equation. Kelsey was right, he wasn't going to get the full picture until he talked to the trainers. And who was going to be more honest than former trainers that no longer had any stake in Galati Fitness. It was time to really listen to what they had to say.

"Well I'll be . . . if it ain't the golden boy himself!"

John spread his arms wide, then bowed regally as he walked into Sin Cycle. For his first stop he had decided to pick a familiar face, a trainer he had helped hire more than twelve years ago—Walter "Walsh" Sinclair.

"I was afraid I might not recognize you, Walsh, but you haven't aged a day . . . you've aged a few decades!"

Walsh smiled and patted his close-cropped grey hair, "I think it looks distinguished. Wife thinks so too."

"The come again now?"

"Had to settle down at some point," Walsh shrugged. "Eventually a lion does have to leave the pride for a lioness."

"Congrats, man." John took a look around. Everything about the store screamed Walsh's personality. The funky colors combined with the raw wood and the stained concrete floor. Cycling jerseys in shadow boxes on the wall. A few bikes inverted on work stands next to a big toolbox. John walked around the space to take it all in. After a moment he let out a low whistle. "This looks more like an old fashioned bike shop than a cycling studio."

"A little bit of both. To be honest, my wife teaches most of the spin classes. I mainly just teach on the weekends when she's racing. I figured there was some unused space in the back here and my garage was getting tight with all my crap." Walsh gestured to his toolboxes all around the shop. "Plus, you know, striking out on your own ain't exactly a gold rush."

"Yeah . . . I feel ya."

Walsh looked up and down at John. "I'm glad to see you! Good to know your brother lets you get out now and then!"

John nodded a little awkwardly; he wasn't quite sure how much to reveal. Walsh jerked a thumb behind him. "You wanna beer or something? I keep a fridge back here."

"No, no. I'm good. I didn't want to take up too much of your time."

"John Hunt turning down a beer. This must not be a purely social visit."

"I wish it were, brother." John leaned against one of the spin bikes. "I wanted to ask you a question. You were a legend at GF. So why did you leave?"

"It was a great run. I'm not denying that. I miss it from time to time. But everyone left. You moved up. I moved on."

"Yeah, I feel ya. But why?"

Walsh looked down at his cuticles. He had the weathered, craggy face of a man who spent a lot of time outdoors, racing through headwinds. "You know. Time to go."

There was a pregnant pause. John felt like he was in front of the group of members again. Except this time there was no Sam to lean on. It was just him. John took a breath and got ready to wing it. He reminded himself to **stay away from expert, biased questions** – anything that was leading or had a predictable answer. John was going to stay curious and find the surprises.

"You know, Walsh, in a lot of ways I envy you. You struck out on your own. You're your own boss now. You've even got a wife. I've got none of that. I was flat-out demoted by Roland. And now I'm sort of going behind his back and trying to figure how and why all these awesome people, members *and* employees, left. And you are one of those awesome people."

Walsh slapped John on the back. "Ah! I knew this wasn't social. I wish I could tell you, but the reason I left is complicated and I'm not sure I'm the guy to help you out. It really wasn't one thing."

John couldn't believe he still couldn't get an answer! He took a couple of breaths. Forget what he thought he knew or how to get it. Focus on what Sam said. Focus on listening. What would she ask him right now? What was the tension point?

"I hear you, man. We don't have to go over the whole thing. Just tell me one thing and I'll get out of your hair—or what's left of it." John smiled.

Walsh laughed and sat down on a stool. "All right, fair enough."

"What was the breaking point? The straw that broke the camel's back?"

Walsh thought about it. And thought about it. He shifted on the stool like he was trying to get comfortable. John thought about interrupting to explain what he meant, but he checked himself. He just waited silently.

Finally, Walsh spoke. "You know what it was, man? It was the one-two punch of the promotional campaign during the holidays three years ago. Things had started to slip a little and I think the Mothership was maybe worried about numbers or something. I don't know. That's your thing, I didn't need to know. But they had the promotion where people could buy up to a year of personal trainer sessions in advance, at an insane rate. It worked out to like 50% off, and it was way cheaper than any of our competitors."

"I remember that!" John said excitedly. "It was a big success at the . . ." He saw a cloud pass over Walsh's usually cheerful face. John put up his hands in a gesture of apology. "Sorry. Go on."

"But it was the way they told us trainers, man. They had some underling come from corporate and tell us that even though they were slashing rates by 50%, we shouldn't worry. They were only going to slash trainer pay by 25%, like they were doing us some favor. They gave us a line about how each trainer would now have so many customers they'd easily make up the difference. But like, I had my classes and limited one-on-one sessions. I was already booked solid, so I didn't get any new customers and I didn't have time for enough customers to make up the 25% difference. It was like they were punishing the most successful trainers for their success. Still, I encouraged my members to get it because it was such a good deal, and I ended up taking a pay cut basically overnight. So that was punch one. It sucked but I stuck around."

"And punch two?"

"That was a couple months later. I guess cutting prices 50% wasn't working out so great, so they started raising prices on all the training services. So then I had to explain to my customers why they had to pay more, but trainer compensation didn't go up one cent. All of the fee increases went directly to the Mothership."

"Jesus, Walsh. I'm sorry."

"Yeah, me too. If GF had been hurting, I would have understood. I'm a team player. I used to love the place. But they weren't. It just felt like we were no longer on the same team . . ." Walsh trailed off.

"So how long after that did you open this?"

"I didn't wait. That day. The very day they announced the price increases, I started looking for spaces to rent. Two weeks later, I found this. The rent was almost too good to be true. Put some wood and some paint in here, got a line of credit to lease those bikes you're currently resting your large butt on, and voila! I was finally working for myself."

"Any regrets?"

"Yeah. A ton. But John, eventually a man has to stand up for himself. It wasn't just the money they were taking. That was my livelihood. And to take it like *that*," Walsh snapped his fingers, "made me realize they could just keep taking it, and there'd be nothing I could do."

"Or they could move you from an executive position to a lowly store manager in under twenty-four hours," he said, as much to himself as to Walsh. "I really appreciate this, Walsh—I just have one last question."

"Shoot."

"Tell me where I can find the rest of the good GF trainers from that time."

"Oh, brother!" Walsh pulled out his cell phone. "You gotta talk to Ainsworth."

"I don't remember him."

"He came on after you left. Probably had the most loyal and devoted following. I was really shocked when he left last year."

Several texts and a couple of hours later, John was at a coffee shop meeting with an unassuming guy in a hoodie. He looked like a cross between a high school science teacher and a crossfitter. Not what John had been expecting.

"Thanks for meeting with me."

"Ya."

"No, it means a lot. You know, a lot of people at GF that I look up to spoke very highly of you."

"Cool."

John felt this was going to be a painful interview if Ainsworth kept his answers to one syllable. He felt himself getting frustrated, but stopped himself. Again, he focused on Sam's advice. *Stay curious.* He decided to ask an open-ended question and then actually listen.

"Ainsworth, how did working at GF make you feel?"

"Feel?" Ainsworth looked off into space. "It was a job."

"And why did it feel like a job?"

Ainsworth squinted at John like he wasn't sure why this strange man was asking about his feelings. "Because that's what being a trainer at GF is. You fill a role."

"Did you feel appreciated?"

He took a sip of his coffee. "No."

"Why did you not feel appreciated?"

Ainsworth blew on his coffee. He was a tough nut to crack and because John had no former friendship with him, he didn't know how hard he could push. Every natural instinct was saying to push harder. Push this guy! But he held back. Hey stayed quiet. Finally, Ainsworth began to speak.

"Look, buddy, I'm sure you mean well . . . I enjoyed GF, but I don't want to insult you. What you did with pushing all the packages and stuff. I know there was a reason for it."

"Huh?" John seemed surprised.

"You know—the add-ons. How we were told to push the add-ons."

"I'm not sure I know what you're talking about. What were the add-ons?"

Ainsworth sighed and leaned back in his chair, balancing it on two legs. "My two big hobbies have always been going to gyms and going to movie theaters. But until I worked as a trainer, I never realized how much they had in common. Movie theaters need to sell concession to make money, since most of the ticket price goes to the studio. The gym is the same way: the protein bars, apparel, vitamins, smoothies, videos, CDs, all that crap, those are like the concessions at the movies. And I was fine with that aspect of the business until you guys forced me to 'close' sales."

"Explain that, please."

He brought the chair back onto all four legs and leaned forward. "So at the movies, when you get a drink and the person behind the counter asks you if you want Milk Duds and you say no, that's the end of it; that guy's getting paid the same either way. That's was the way it used to be at GF too. But when they changed trainer compensation, they also added all these add-ons that we had to sell. Before, if I thought a DVD or stretching band would help my client, I'd suggest they look into buying it. But then it became that instead of just training members, we had to sell at least ten DVDs a month, or fifteen stretching bands a month, and if we didn't then we didn't get all of our incentive pay. So naturally, trainers started finding extra things to sell to members, even if they didn't need it or had already bought a lot of other things. We went from being trainers whose responsibility was to our clients, to glorified concession workers selling them crap they didn't need."

John thought back to the executive meetings at GF. He remembered how various department heads wanted help pushing their latest project, apparel, exercise DVDs, even John's GF branded energy drinks. They all talked about incentivizing trainers and employees to push this out, and it made perfect sense—of course trainers were the most natural and trustworthy salespeople! But now he realized that no one in those meetings had ever questioned how the trainers themselves might react or how upselling impacted the customer. Huge blind spots on both fronts! And the policy had only given a short-term boost to revenue, and had had a pretty negative impact on loyalty.

They'd just taken both the trainers and their members for granted. A sick knot was forming in his stomach. He was complicit in this and he'd had no idea.

"Tell me more. Please," John said, almost imploringly. He didn't have to make a conscious effort to listen anymore; he just wanted to hear Ainsworth's story.

"It made me feel cheap. It would be like if you were told your job was to sell Milk Duds at the movies and then because they weren't selling enough, you were told to go harass people in their seats until they bought your daily quota. That's what it felt like—like we were being ordered to harass customers and if we didn't obey, then we didn't get paid."

"That sounds terrible."

"And, like, it was never *enough*, either. I was good at selling things but after a couple months there are only so many DVDs a person can buy. And the members hated it too. After a while, they stopped trusting my recommendations, and so they stopped trusting me altogether. As a trainer, you and the client have to be on the same team, but this compensation plan was pitting us against them. I remember I'd actually get *annoyed* when a client didn't buy whatever protein shake I was pitching. That was my breaking point."

He took a deep breath to calm himself and checked his watch. "You can't keep selling popcorn to people who already have popcorn. That's what GF didn't understand." Ainsworth got up. "Sorry to cut this short, but I need to head back to work."

"Not at all—thank you so much. What gym are you working at now?"

"I'm not." Ainsworth smiled and pointed to a small movie theater across the street. "I manage an art-house movie theater."

Suddenly Ainsworth's analogy made so much sense.

Night had fallen, and John felt like he needed to get in a workout. It had been an insane day, and he wanted to burn off all the excess energy. It was after nine p.m. when he got back to Zero, and the day crew had all gone home.

He'd spent hours shuttling around the city, and had managed to talk to six former employees of Galati Fitness. Not surprisingly, a lot of people who had left GF in the past couple of years had left with a bad taste in their mouth. He played their stories over and over as he muscled his way through a series of squats. How could they have taken the trainers for granted like that? John was getting ready to do some box jumps when he caught the eye of a new trainer whose name he couldn't remember. The instant his feet touched the top of the box, it hit him: he'd completely forgotten about the current trainers, the people who had stuck with GF through it all. He scanned the gym. The problem was, only one evening trainer at Zero had experience, and that trainer was Bek.

Bek was the night-time trainer who worked at a car dealership on the weekends and always seemed to have one or two business ideas he was "working on." Bek was a legend at GF, but not in the good way. More in the way that some people just acquire legend status by sticking around for a long time, like Matthew McConaughey's character in *Dazed and Confused*. To this point, John's only interaction with Bek had been a couple of hellos. But now, it was like John could hear Sam whispering in his ear, **"you can't just solicit feedback from the people you like**."

"Heyyy, Bek, what's going on!" John approached him as he was re-tightening some TRX straps.

"What's up, kid?" Bek called everybody who was younger than him 'kid.' Maybe other people found it endearing, but John definitely didn't.

"Not much. Just working out and realized we haven't gotten an opportunity to chat."

Bek's upper lip twitched in a brief flicker of contempt. "Mm-hmm. Sure, kid. What do you want?"

Fine, thought John. He wasn't here to be flattered, he was here to learn. "Are you happy, Bek?"

Bek's eyes bugged, and he looked at John with profound suspicion. "Oh of course. Of course. Boss is asking if I'm happy. Look at this smile." Bek gave an overly big obvious fake smile. "Don't I look happy?"

"I don't know, Bek, but I'm genuinely asking. I've talked to some former trainers about how the Mothership cut back pay, forced sales on customers they didn't need, and made add-ons required for compensation."

"This ain't exactly breaking news, kid."

"Humor me. I want to know. Do you feel like that's true?"

Bek narrowed his eyes. Clearly, he didn't trust John in the least.

"Look, I get that you don't know me," said John, finally. "So don't answer for my sake, answer for Mr. G's."

Bek rolled his eyes. "That old fart? Fine. What you said is all true."

"But is that it?"

"Well, after Mr. G left, you and your brother kept changing the metrics of how we'd get paid. First, it was cutting the base pay."

"Yeah. Walsh mentioned that."

"Oh, you talked to Walsh?" Hearing this seemed to loosen Bek up a little. "Yeah, he left right after that, and at first I just liked getting all his old clients. Seniority, baby. And I thought it couldn't get worse. But it did. Because while they did up the pay based on incentives, they kept changing what 'total dollars brought in' meant. First, it was all encompassing, so if I had a member renew and bring in another member and they both got a training session and then a class and rented a locker, I got a nice little cut of all that. And life was good. But then you guys decided God forbid the trainers make too much money, so you kept adjusting the metrics of exactly *what* stream of revenue counted towards our compensation and what streams didn't."

"I'm listening."

"So suddenly, I go from getting a percentage of everything I sell, to no longer getting a percentage from the class. Then you changed from giving us a percentage of merchandise sales, to giving a base bonus if we sell X amount of each item. And now if we don't hit the base, we don't get jack."

"Yeah. A trainer named Ainsworth mentioned that too."

"Well, did he or Walsh mention what the Mothership did last year?" John shook his head. Bek was enjoying letting John have it—this was cathartic for him. It wasn't fun to bear the brunt of Bek's attack but by listening, John was gaining insights.

"So the biggest pot of gold has always been renewals. Ask every trainer at GF. Every single one. That's where the most money is because the members are no longer joining on ridiculous low January joiner prices and we can lock them into a four-figure contract like that." Richard snapped his fingers. "But last year the Mothership said we were no longer getting compensation based on renewals. They didn't care about my members anymore. No, all they cared about was *new* members."

"Seriously?" John was genuinely shocked. Being at the Mothership and away from the gyms' everyday hustle and bustle, he didn't realize how much things had changed. John knew that new members were a strong priority for the management team, but he never thought about the consequences of their initiatives on the trainers. They'd accidentally devalued the trainers because they hadn't taken the time to learn how the new programs were being received in the field. No wonder Bek was so mad!

Bek was off on a full-blown rant now, and John continued to listen. Bek had grievance after grievance, but nothing stuck with John quite like the way Bek described the compensation being changed. John understood that all the "innovations" he'd pushed were just as responsible for the changes that were driving trainers away as anyone on the executive team. They didn't just have huge blind spots in terms of the customer experience, he had uncovered some equally-menacing blind spots in the way their trainers were being treated, and how new programs were being rolled out.

John was so deep in thought after his conversation with Bek that he drove straight past his apartment and all the way back to his old hotel. He didn't realize his mistake until he walked into the lobby and realized the elevator bank was not where he'd expected it to be. By the time he finally got back to his apartment, it was after eleven.

He was sitting on his couch, barely paying attention to the TV, and debating what to do. He hadn't felt this *tired* in years. It was probably time to go to bed. Then his phone pinged. John looked down and saw a text message from an unknown number with an unfamiliar area code.

Have any more useful conversations?

Yeah. He texted back. Sorry, who is this?

Someone with excellent taste in footwear.

Startled, John almost dropped his phone.

What are you doing up at this hour?

Standing outside your door.

All of a sudden, John was wide awake.

CHAPTER SIXTEEN

SAM STOOD IN FRONT OF JOHN'S APARTMENT DOOR, WAITING
for him to see the text she'd just sent. The six-pack of beer she
was holding was getting heavy.

The apartment was in one of those purgatorial complexes
where she'd spent as much time finding the right apartment
building as she did getting to the right door. All the doors were
a beige that made other beiges look flamboyant by comparison.
She had finally found the right door, but in her head, she was
still doing the mental math of what she was actually doing here
at eleven p.m.

The neighbor's door directly across the hall facing John's
door had a little ceramic gnome guarding it. Sam figured the
tenant had put it there to add a personal touch. It had the opposite effect, though; the ludicrous little gnome's presence made
the rest of the hallway seem even more grim and sterile.

She told herself she was here because she'd been finding this
GF situation fun. She had a personal stake in it because Zero
was only a couple minutes from her house and she liked the
people there. She didn't want to have to go find a whole new
gym if something should happen to this one. But Sam knew the
truth was, she couldn't help herself. She knew her time was

valuable—her girlfriends kept telling her to stop taking on pro bono consulting projects, when she could be charging them out the ears. But time and time again, she found herself unable to resist. Whether it was helping her massage therapist with her marketing plan and scheduling technology, or helping her carpenter develop a referral program, she simply could not leave a business problem unsolved. That was her happy place.

The mistake with GF was thinking that it would be a quick problem to solve. That GF's woes were only superficial. But no, the more advice she gave, it seemed like the more advice Mr. G and John needed.

She tried not to dwell on the fact that she hadn't gone to John's hotel room that first night because she was just so enthralled with hearing about his business problems. No matter how much she tried to talk herself out it, she was attracted to him.

But that was all secondary now. Maybe there'd be time for all that after, but right now, she was here to help John. That's what friends did.

The door swung open, and John was standing there goggle-eyed. Sam waltzed in like she owned the place. Just because she had internal self-doubt didn't mean she was about to let John see it.

She flopped onto his sofa, cracked open a beer, and offered him one. She had expected John's apartment to be spartan, but this was next level. Not a single picture hung on the walls, not one single flower wilting in a vase.

"I love what you've done with the place," Sam joked. "I can see you've been nesting."

"Don't want strangers like you getting too comfortable," he quipped. "Next thing you know they might want to spend the night."

Once again she was struck by how easily, how comfortably they flirted. Sam settled into the sofa, and John sat down across from her in an armchair that looked to be from the Eisenhower administration.

Immediately, he started in. "You'll never believe how successful these interviews were."

"Whoa. No small talk?"

John shook his head. "Not when I've got bigger talk. I've found some pretty juicy low hanging fruit."

"That's great! Listening tends to do that."

"My gut says to go talk to Roland. To tell him everything that we've discovered and hope that he lets us make some pretty big changes."

"And you think that's going to work?"

John snorted. "About as well as fitting three weightlifters into a two-man tent."

Sam almost spit her beer out laughing. "I'll take your word for it on that one. But wait, what's your angle here? Why do you want to bring this to Roland if you think Roland is going to say no?"

"It's not just Roland. It's the current environment over there. Nobody wants to rock the boat. For a gym built on creativity and innovation, it was difficult to implement even the smallest things I wanted to try."

"Explain." Sam had switched into listening mode. It really was true, she reflected, after a while it did come naturally. Sure enough, it caused John to lean back and get comfortable on his deflated old armchair.

He cracked his beer. "When I first came on as the director of innovation, we had a loyalty card. You know, one of those paper cards that people got stamped to earn rewards. Like when you buy bagels or donuts, except we tailored it for training sessions."

"Yeah. I remember those. I used to have one I think. It's probably floating around an old purse."

"Probably next to your Blockbuster card," John chuckled. "Anyway, we had no idea who was getting them stamped, or how they were using the card, and we were missing all these opportunities to nudge customers to do more with us. It was the perfect innovation project. We could turn the paper card into an app that people could just have on their phones, and we could devise all kinds of new uses for it. Add a QR code and boom! We could incorporate it into everything. From checking in to getting discounts on classes. So I do this big presentation to the executive team thinking it's a home run and the first question I get, the very first one, was how many people would be affected by the change. I told them I hoped everyone would—and immediately I could tell that answer scared them. The idea of actual *change* in the way we did business was terrifying. So they formed a committee and invited every department head that could be affected to that committee and here we are, three years later and the only thing we've been able to accomplish is moving from a paper loyalty card to a plastic one, and no other changes."

Sam swigged her beer and belched decorously. "Honestly, that makes sense."

"You agree with them?" John leaned forward.

"Not agree with them, but I'm not as shocked as you are. **Most existing processes inside of a company are structured to safeguard the company, which is at odds with innovation and trying new things.**"

"Okay, so then how does any company innovate?"

"They ask **Essential Curiosity Question #3: What can I** *test*? Testing helps us de-risk big ideas before investing. So, of course when you told them every member would be affected, they freaked out. I mean, it sounds pretty risky, right?"

"I guess it did."

"**The best way to prove the value of an idea, John, is to conduct some small experiments to dramatically reduce the risk.** You can't just stop being curious when you think you've found a problem worth solving. You have to **be just as curious about finding a solution** that will actually create value for the company. You don't know if a loyalty app would decrease attrition or drive overall sales, right? These are just assumptions you had. You were guessing. Just like you thought removing all the fees would keep members from leaving."

John sipped his beer. He leaned back, which she knew was supposed to project confidence, but she was also getting to know John well enough to know when he was faking it. Right now his body was projecting comfort, but his face was etched with dejection. She'd seen it often—it was what normally happened when someone asked Sam for feedback. They'd expect her to confirm their opinions, but instead got the ice-water bucket of truth dumped on their heads.

Not that it bothered her—that look meant she was doing something right. John needed this talk and she was feeling more comfortable. Her unease at the door was fading as she grew more worked up about Galati Fitness's problems. This was what she loved to do, and she had plenty more ice buckets where that one had come from.

"So getting back to what you can do right now about all these problems you've found. I would avoid what you've done before. You can't go to Roland now and tell him your big discoveries and expect him to do anything about it. Remember, he's worried about innovation theater. He's worried that you may have misheard the customers, that your hypothesis about the employees is all wrong. He's worried about you spending all kinds of money to chase these problems without any kind of ROI. That's why **presenting a problem without some kind of a tested solution inside of a big organization is a recipe for delay.**"

John heaved a giant sigh. "Sam, are you sure you're not working for Roland? He didn't put you on the payroll, did he?"

"I don't know if he can afford me," Sam laughed. "But believe it or not, I know where he's coming from. I used to have Roland's job and after a while, I informally started referring to myself as the C-E-NO. There was no shortage of ideas out there, but those ideas carried risk. **My most important job was to guide and encourage the folks that had all those ideas without saying yes to every one.** So asking how we could test the ideas allowed us to place our bets on the ideas that were most likely to pay off."

John put his hands on the back of his head and leaned back, deep in thought. Sam drained the last of her beer.

"But what can I do about this at the store level if compensation and incentives are happening at headquarters?" Sam could tell John was racking his brain.

"You can start by getting me another beer," she said, waggling her empty bottle. With a disgruntled kick of his leg, John scooted the beer across the floor to her sofa.

"Thanks for the effort," Sam said. "Look, **everyone can do something to test an idea,** John. Everyone in the company has different resources or latitudes to be able to perform an experiment. They just don't think it's possible . . . bottle opener?" This beer was a different top than the others. That's what you got with an assortment pack. John pointed to the side of the fridge. The bottle opener was in the shape of a flexed arm. It was about the only cute thing John had in the whole apartment.

Sam came back to the couch and sprawled out, making herself more comfortable. "I know you want to go racing right to the solution. But don't stop being curious now. **Be just as curious about solving the problem as you were about figuring out what the problem was**. Right now you have a hypothesis, and it's really risky and expensive to implement. Can you imagine how much it would cost to change everyone's compensation and incentive structure company-wide? That sounds crazy to do on a hunch. You need experiments . . ." Sam paused to think about the best way to phrase it. "You want Roland to be thinking of the *opportunity*, not the risk, and the best way to do that is to **make small bets that pay off**."

John ambled to the kitchen and brought back a bag of popcorn, but when he returned, he sat down on the couch next to Sam. Uh oh. Laying down on the couch might have been a bad idea. She at first pretended like it was nothing. She kept talking business.

"Companies have a bias toward planning, and researching, and safeguarding. Innovators have a bias towards action. I'm not saying you need to do crazy things that will get you fired. I'm saying simple experiments that prove that this idea will create value. It's got to be something where you can see results in a week or two."

John nodded, leaned forward to take a handful of popcorn, and shifted closer to her. She continued to talk.

"And don't feel like you need to do all of this on your own! **Essential Curiosity Question #4: How can you engage others to achieve your goal?** Who can help you come up with these experiments? Don't just put everything on your shoulders . . ."

John interrupted her with a kiss. And for a moment, Sam let herself kiss him back. A beer and a half was just enough to lower her inhibitions. Her body was saying *go for it* but her mind was reaching for the emergency brake. After a few more moments of feeling his surprisingly velvety and slightly salty lips, her mind won and she pulled away and sat back on the couch.

"You know, I feel like you're missing out on some awesome business lessons here."

John smiled. "Sure, but I need a study break." He went in for another kiss; this time Sam dodged it.

"Look, I'm not sure if this is a good idea."

He looked at her confused, like a puppy who doesn't understand why he's not allowed on the bed. She knew the question that was coming up and she needed a couple of swigs of beer to get ready to answer.

"What about that first night together?"

Sam shook her head. "I hate to burst your bubble, big guy, but barely anything happened."

"What? Then how did your shoes wind up under my bed?"

"I did come back to your hotel room, but all you wanted to do was talk. I couldn't shut you up. We sat on that little balcony looking out at the highway and talked."

"About anything in particular?"

"Well . . . you kept telling me about this girl you had broken up with."

"Oh nooo," John wailed, hanging his head in disbelief. "Tell me I didn't."

"And at first I thought it was just normal breaking-up blues and that you needed to get some things out of your system. But you kept going on and on about her. And once we worked our way through the mini bar and it became obvious that nothing was going to happen, I left."

"Kelsey? I told you about the breakup with Kelsey?"

Before Sam could answer, there was a knock at the door. John looked at her quizzically, then at the clock. "What is this, a flophouse? It's eleven-thirty!"

Another knock, louder and more urgent. John slowly got up from the couch and walked towards the door. Sam sat up and swung her feet off the couch. It just felt like the right move.

John slowly opened the door but practically shrieked when he saw who was on the other side, "Kelsey? Wha . . . what are you doing here?" Sam couldn't quite make out the response. She heard bits and pieces: ". . . courage to talk . . .", ". . . apartment number . . .", ". . . can I come in?"

If at that moment, a passing asteroid had decided to make a detour and obliterate the whole earth, that would have been all right with Sam.

John was doing his best to keep her in the hallway but Sam knew it was likely only a matter of time before she came into the apartment. Should she hide? Try to leave? Lock herself in the bathroom?

John tried to say something about it not being a good time and that they could talk tomorrow, but that just seemed to embolden Kelsey. She said some things loudly in the hallway and shoved past him into the apartment and started looking around. When her eyes met Sam's, it was obvious she had confirmed her worst suspicions. All Sam could do was give a frail little wave.

"I'll, uh, I'll just go," Sam managed to say.

"No!" Kelsey shouted. She tried to compose herself before speaking again. "Clearly, I've interrupted. I'll let myself out."

And before anyone else had a chance to say anything, she

zoomed out of the apartment. John made a half-hearted attempt to call after her, but she was already at the stairs, not bothering to wait for the elevator.

He turned towards Sam, hopelessly perplexed, still trying to make sense of what just happened.

Sam walked towards the door. "I think I should go."

"Are you sure?"

"I don't want to get in the middle of anything."

"There's no middle, Sam. We're broken up! I don't know what that was . . . but there's nothing to get in the middle of!"

"Goodnight, John." She had no interest in arguing, or in drama. This had been a mistake. As the elevator doors closed, she took a deep breath. Hadn't her New Year's resolution been to be more mindful of relationships, both hers and those of other people? Stupid non-binding worthless resolutions.

For all her wizardry with business, it wasn't until very recently that she'd realized her own "expertise" had sabotaged one relationship after another. She'd meant for this year to be different. She wanted to stay with John—win him, even, as stupid as it sounded. But it didn't feel right. No matter what John said about the situation, she'd seen how he talked about Kelsey when he was drunk. There was something still there.

Damn feelings.

CHAPTER
SEVENTEEN

JOHN ARRIVED LATE AT ZERO THE NEXT MORNING FEELING very much like the offensive line of the Miami Dolphins had spent the entire night clog-dancing on his head. Polishing off all the beer in his house tended to have that effect on him. Kelsey and Mr. G were already waiting for him in Studio 2. John was hoping to have some time to talk to Kelsey before the three of them were scheduled to meet, but now that was not likely to happen.

Kelsey was leaning against the wall. She avoided all eye contact with John. If Mr. G noticed Kelsey's unease, he didn't let on. He grabbed a big red stability ball from the corner of the room and sat on it. He looked up expectantly at John.

"So? What was so exciting that I had to cancel golf this morning?"

"Since when do you golf?"

"Since I got fat and retired. Let's move it, John."

"Yes, can we please just get this done?" Kelsey snapped.

John decided to ignore whatever was happening between the two of them. He would focus on Mr. G and try to patch things up with Kelsey later. "So yesterday was pretty great. Really, one of the most enlightening days of my career. I feel like we're actually finally breaking through the rock and getting to the gold."

Just then Randy came in with coffees. He handed Mr. G's his first and then one to Kelsey and then finally a coffee for John. John was trying to hide the surprise on his face about Randy joining the meeting, but it must have been pretty obvious because Mr. G cackled, "I put Randy to good use this morning getting us some proper nutrients." Mr. G jabbed a thumb at Randy. "I'm beginning to like him, you know! Thanks for sticking around, Randy!"

Randy grinned; he had movie-star teeth. "Thanks for asking, Mr. G." Then he looked at John, who shrugged his shoulders. If Mr. G wanted Randy around, there was no harm in getting another's person's perspective.

John went on to explain to the group what he had discovered from his listening tour. About how both members and trainers were suffering from trainers being forced to push products. About how much trainers hated the constant changes in their compensation, and the sense that the goal posts were always moving. About GF coming in between the important relationship between trainer and member. He almost said, "like an unwanted third wheel," but saw Kelsey and caught himself. How they needed to focus on that relationship and make it better. Finally, after nearly an hour of talking, John clasped his hands together. "So, that's the data."

By now, Kelsey had come off the wall and was sitting on a yoga mat. "Okay. So we have the data. How do we solve it?" She meant it too. Getting to a decision with purpose was one of her more admirable qualities. No matter what she was going through personally, she was always there for GF.

Mr. G, who had been suspiciously quiet the entire time,

jumped in. "I'll tell you what we can do. We start with . . ." Whereupon he launched into a catalogue of solutions, carefully pointing out what used to work when he was in charge, and insisting that they return to those old ways.

This time, though, John saw these solutions for what they were—he felt like he was getting déjà vu. It was no different from when Mr. G decided the à la carte fees were the problem. Suddenly a light went off in John's head. **Question 4: How can you engage others?** John looked at Randy, "Mr. G. What if we try a different perspective and ask the Randys of GF what they would do?"

Randy blanched. "Uhh . . . I'm not exactly an expert at all this business stuff."

John came over to Randy and slapped him on the back, causing him to wobble on his rubber stability ball. "Damn right. You're not an expert. That's why we need you. Randy, how quickly do you think you can get a handful of trainers here?"

Randy rubbed his head. "Give me a few minutes?" He took off towards the door.

Mr. G wasn't excited about the direction, but he was open to it. And for the first time in his GF career, John didn't feel all the pressure to come up with the big idea. Since the trainers were the ones who personally felt the problems, they would be in a much better place to help craft a solution. He could hear Sam in his ear, **"You can't be curious by yourself. Your solution is going to be a lot more powerful if you co-create it with those who will be affected."**

Half an hour and two more black coffees later, John was feeling more like himself, there were five trainers in the room, including Bek. They looked a little bored but not that surprised— they were used to getting yanked around at GF and it seemed like some of them were bracing for bad news. John quickly sought to calm them.

"Hi, everyone—first of all, don't worry! This meeting is not to announce any changes. I'm not getting rid of anyone or cutting anyone's hours or changing pay schedule. Instead, I . . . we need your help."

"Oh boy." Bek rolled his eyes, "What's the catch?"

"Yeah, what's this about?" said another trainer, glancing nervously back and forth between Randy and John.

"No catch, Bek. Not at all." John gathered his thoughts. He needed to do something to keep this from becoming a complaining session. He needed to take charge. The first thing to do was be up front with them. He gave them an abbreviated version of the findings he'd given to Mr. G and Kelsey, holding nothing back.

When John was done explaining what he'd uncovered, he turned to Bek specifically, but addressed all the trainers. "So now I have a pretty simple question for you: how can we improve the trainer-member relationship? Really, we want to hear your ideas. No judgment. No attribution. No bad ideas, but we have to do something. **We need to find a way of testing whether this is as much of an opportunity as we think.**" The power of Sam Donovan was strong within John now. "Everyone can do something to test an idea. **Everyone in the company has different resources to be able to perform an experiment.** So what can we do?"

"Jesus," Bek laughed, "You're asking us how to save the company?"

Mr. G, Kelsey, and John all looked at each other and nodded. "Kind of, yeah. What would you do?"

"Well just change the compensation for trainers to straight

cash! The way it used to be. Done! Can I go home now?" Bek said.

John grimaced.

Kelsey jumped in. "We can't do anything about compensation. It's all controlled centrally now. Even if John wanted to, there's no way he could tap into the system and change compensation on his own. What about more local ideas? Things we can implement here at this gym?"

One woman piped up. "Well, we could call old members."

"I'm not calling sweaty Larry! That's not my job!" Another trainer protested.

"No, no, no," John interrupted. "Remember, there are no bad ideas. I want us to try a number of different things. Maybe some people who want to call old members do that, and people who don't want to, try something completely different? What if we experiment around what those calls sound like?"

John got some head nods. "Okay, so what else?"

"How about the way we talk to members?"

John was about to jump in and say he hoped they'd figured that out by now, but instead he channeled his inner Sam and pulled back. "Explain," he asked the trainer.

"Like instead of doing all the upsell with the shakes and the t-shirts and the electronics, what about we train them how best we feel they need it."

"You mean like no longer requiring the tablets?" John asked.

"Oh *God*, yes," the trainer cried. "Let me throw those out!"

"Whoa! Let's not throw them out, but yes, I like that idea. We'll consider whether to make the tablets optional. What else? Keep them coming."

The trainer farthest from John spoke up. "We could allow members to bring a friend for free."

"Yeah! Like tag along during their workout!" someone called. "We could also keep a board of our outstanding members. Like who's lost the most weight or done the most box jumps that week."

"Fantastic, I love it. Like a member spotlight." John rubbed his hands together—this was getting good.

The trainer farthest from John spoke up again. "Well, if we're going to do a board and a spotlight, why don't we do a competition? Have members compete against each other—"

"–While tracking their progress!" Mr. G leapt in. "We used to always list the top weightlifters! We could go back to that! We should have never left it!"

"Oh, for crying out loud," Bek groaned. "You're all missing the point."

John turned to Bek. He'd had it about up to here with his negativity. "And the point is . . . ?"

"If we're going to have a competition, it shouldn't be between members. It should be between us."

"Us?" said the one in the back. "Like we should have a trainer competition?"

Suddenly Bek got a little meek with the spotlight on him. "Well . . . not a fight to the death—I'm old, I'll die first—but a friendly competition to see who helps members the most."

Kelsey was nodding her head furiously. "Okay, okay! I like this! I could easily come up with five categories, set a baseline, then track performance over the median during that timeframe."

Half of the words Kelsey'd used shot over John's head like swallows on the wing. He wasn't a math guy, but the fact that she was excited meant a lot. "Okay. So you're saying it's possible. But what would be the point of the competition?"

"Pride!" Mr. G interjected.

Pride. That was the one thing that all the trainers he'd spoken to had lost. They'd all felt humiliated by the new schemes, just like he had when Roland had banished him. Maybe there was something in this. "I can see this working," John said. "Maybe some kind of prize if I can swing it. I promise to try."

"Hold on, hold on. We have to set goals first," Kelsey interrupted. "Ones based on individual client goals, not GF goals. How about this: starting today, each trainer has their clients write down their personal goals. In one month, we ask every member how much their trainer or class instructor helped them get closer to that goal. And whichever trainer has the best score, wins."

There was a chorus of "Oh yeah!" and "I could do that" that quickly devolved into "look out, chumps!" and "you couldn't train a fish to swim!"

"I like it. No, no–I more than like it. I love it!" Mr. G cried. "It's good. It's cheap. It's doable. It's fast. It seems to address actual members' concerns. It seems to address trainers' concerns."

"Absolutely," beamed John. "But it's only one idea. Let's keep going."

So they did. For another hour. The trainers were a lot more engaged, but no idea seemed to stick like the competition. As the creative juices were beginning to ebb, John glanced over at Kelsey and she flashed him a smile back. It seemed forced, but at least she was trying.

John thought this might be his opening. As the trainers were filing out of the studio, already talking trash to each other about how they were going to win, he came up to Kelsey. "Hey, you got a minute to talk? I just wanted to . . ."

She wasn't going to let him finish. "Gotta take off for the airport! Sorry, John—but I'll be helping from the Mothership!" She started heading towards the door. "Good luck with this!" And just like that, she was gone again.

CHAPTER
EIGHTEEN

A MONTH LATER, KELSEY WALKED THROUGH THE GLASS DOORS of GF Zero and immediately she could tell something was different. It was one month into "the Challenge," as the team had decided to call it. She'd already seen the numbers, but she could tell by the sound alone: kettlebells thumped on mats; weights slid and clanked on Cybex machines; jump ropes whisked the floor; treadmills hummed at high speed; ellipticals whirred; trainers barked encouragement at customers. *This* was how a gym should sound, she thought.

When Kelsey had first arrived at Zero, none of the trainers had seemed especially approachable or friendly. Now though, walking around, it was common to hear trainers ask members some variation of, "What do you want to get out of this? Are you working towards anything specific?" And the most important part was that they were listening. They weren't just swanning around going "Hey! Everything good here? Great. See you later." They were definitely more engaged.

She walked by a pair of trainers she recognized who were dialing no-show customers. It was one of the suggestions she helped turn into a test: calling people who had not checked in in a while to see what problems they had with the gym and whether they could offer a free training session to get them back on track. Kelsey had been sending new call sheets for the trainers almost every day.

The trainers looked like they were working in concert around the gym. They approached people if they looked confused or needed a spot, or just to hand them a towel if they needed one. They weren't pushy, they were just attentive.

Kelsey was back to share her data with Mr. G and John. Mr. G insisted on doing it in person. And with the insight team still hanging on by a string, Zero felt like the most exciting thing she had going on, so she didn't mind. Both Mr. G and John knew the numbers were good, but she came with all the breakdowns of the experiments that were making the biggest difference and the overall improvement numbers.

The evidence was hard to deny. Zero was quickly becoming an outlier in the system by significantly reducing customer attrition. The Challenge was yielding significant results.

The fact that the idea had come from the trainers in the first place set it far apart from every other new program implementation she'd seen at GF. Kelsey had finally realized the problem: normally, a program, usually a solution to something that wasn't broken, would be handed down from the fourth floor as if written on two stone tablets atop Mount Sinai. But back down at the bottom of Mount Sinai—that is, at the actual gyms—implementation was a whole lot more complicated.

She'd been a part of many of these programs the Mothership had cooked up and foisted onto trainers and individual stores. For instance, the tablets. She'd been on the team that had sold the fourth floor on the tablets, developed the unique software for them, gone to individual test gyms to teach trainers how to use them, and then eventually became a full-throated supporter of rolling them out at every GF.

And yet, she realized, not once had she actually asked trainers what it was like to use the tablets. Or even better, if they *needed* the tablets. Or whether the tablets improved the trainer or member experience. They just thrust them into trainers' hands and said, "this is how you do your job now." No wonder the data had been garbage and trainers were forever apologizing that their tablets were "broken."

Now, though, the trainers were not only excited, they were engaged. She and John and Mr. G had finally given them a voice and they were using it. Each one had made his or her contribution to devising The Challenge and they were taking it seriously. **Involving the trainers in coming up with the solution did wonders for increasing their buy-in and engagement.** As she walked around the periphery of the gym, Kelsey felt a kind of deep satisfaction growing in her. She hated to say it, but the Buddhist monks could never have given her this feeling.

The time away from Zero had also been a good distraction from the awkwardness between her and John. They'd been working together, but at a reassuring distance. No deep conversations about life or how each of them was doing. It had stayed professional, and Kelsey even started to believe she'd gotten over him. It was like slowly detoxing from John.

After the breakup, when things had gone radio-silent, she'd built John up in her mind. But a month of working in close proximity to the real John had comprehensively exploded her imaginary John. The real one dressed shabbily and wore dirty sneakers and didn't use proper grammar all the time. Every day was a little reminder that yes, John was human. Some days made her think the breakup was for the best; other days, it made her ache for him even more.

Standing in the middle of the gym, Kelsey self-assessed how she felt about the John situation and decided the pain had soothed, like the way a headache fades after a fistful of aspirin. She was ready to go find him to talk about the numbers. She scanned the gym and saw John working on his plank in the back of a studio.

He was angled away from the door and as she approached she could hear him hissing to himself, "Focus, John! Get serious!"

Kelsey almost snorted with laughter, but he was clearly struggling. She saw him sag and then try to get up, then move his legs apart, then back together. He didn't notice her and shifted to breathing out in a really loud way, like a congested buffalo. He was in his own world. Kelsey had been there probably a full minute when John finally thumped into the mat. That was when he finally noticed she was in the room.

"Kelsey!" He got up—slowly, painfully—to say hello.

"Sorry. Didn't mean to disturb you. Whatcha get?"

John dabbed his head with a towel. "Six minutes and ten seconds."

Kelsey's eyebrows raised a bit. "Wow. I'm impressed!"

"Nah. I had seven minutes in me."

"Still six minutes. Not bad, right?"

John frowned. "It's not enough to beat Roland, that's for sure."

"Roland can do more?"

John nodded. "Last I checked." He looked back down at his watch. "Mind if I do one more?"

"Again? Aren't you tired?"

"It's something new I'm trying. Following up my max plank

with shorter planks. I talked to this guy who planked competitively and asked him what I might be missing, and he told me about maxing out and then trying again. So that's what I'm doing." John got down on his knees and elbows and lifted off the mat. **"If you want better results, you need to ask better questions**."

There was a mat laying close to him. Kelsey was curious how long she could keep up. She threw down her jacket and purse and got into a plank herself. "Like what type of questions?" she asked.

"Like **what are your blind spots? What are the things you think you're doing well that you really aren't**?" John gazed at her. "Just watching you now I can see that your butt is too low and you're up too far on your elbows. And did you know that strengthening your glutes is super important for a good plank? That was a total blind spot to me. I never would have figured it out on my own."

"Huh." Kelsey wanted to keep the conversation away from her butt. She shifted her elbows and the subject. "So pretty exciting about the numbers, right?" She was struggling to talk and keep her form. "It's *way* better than when you tried removing all those fees."

"One minute," John grunted. "I'm pumped about these numbers and the trainers have a lot of pride. But I just don't want us to get cocky. I love Mr. G and you love Mr. G, but he is pretty addicted to being right and he kind of steamrolled everyone else to get his way that first time around. What's funny is that looking back, that's the very thing I was trying to fight against at the Mothership. We thought Roland and his management team weren't listening to customers or employees and just launching new ideas and so what did we do? We came here and didn't listen to customers or employees and just launched new ideas."

"Pretty ironic." Kelsey shifted her weight and a blue flare of pain shot down the left side of her abdomen. This was tough. She went back into bad elbow position but she didn't care because it felt better. "I hate this already, John. How do you know if you're asking the right questions?"

"Ah," John smiled. **"You know if you're being curious if you're finding surprises. Like punch-in-the-gut, how-could-I-have-been-so-blind surprises."**

"I've got a punch in the gut right now. Wait—are you lifting a hand off the ground? Son of a—"

John laughed. The first real laugh in the conversation. Kelsey knew it was his real laugh too. She missed that laugh. Another twinge, this one higher than her abs.

John didn't seem to notice. "You know," he went on, "we preach at the gym that **if it doesn't challenge you, it doesn't change you**. If you aren't uncomfortable, then you are not improving. And . . ."

Before John could finish, Kelsey fell. John looked at his watch.

"Two minutes and thirty-three seconds. Hey, look—way better than my first try! But there's one more thing. **We need to keep experimenting. Even if something feels like it's working, we can't stop being curious and looking for ways to do it even better**. That's the only way to make sure you never stop improving."

At three minutes, John gently lowered his knees and sat up. Kelsey envied the fact that he had been more graceful than her. He looked at her and smiled. So far, they'd kept it all professional. Well, for the most part.

"So, Obi-Wan, are we talking about getting better at planks or saving our company?"

"Both, I think. This stuff applies to anything you want to improve: problems you want to solve, goals you want to reach, relationships you want to fi—" The words had fallen out of his mouth before he could catch himself.

Kelsey looked away, her good mood evaporating.

John reached out gingerly. "Hey, I know it's been hard, Kels. It's not easy for me either."

"You've got a lot of good ideas these days. You must be hanging out with Sam a lot lately." She just couldn't help herself. Talking about Sam was the last thing she wanted to do, but it just came out.

"Oh come on, now," he said.

Kelsey scowled. "Oh come on yourself, John. Listen to yourself . . . all this stuff you're saying, it's all her."

"Kelsey . . ."

"No, no. It's all right. I know we're broken up. You're free to see whoever you want."

"Kels."

Kelsey didn't want to lose it in front of John. She seized her things and made for the door.

This was not how things were supposed to go.

She heard John's phone ring as she was walking out.

"Kelsey, wait! It's Roland!"

Kelsey froze. There was no way she was going to miss this conversation.

CHAPTER NINETEEN

ROLAND HAD JUST FINISHED HIS PLANKS. HE PREFERRED TO do them outside, in a park, but it was raining this morning. So instead, he was using his own private gym at his house. "Private gym" made it sound a lot more glamorous than it was—it was a treadmill, an elliptical, some yoga mats, a full-length mirror, and three TVs showing the latest stock news.

When Roland planked indoors, he usually propped a tablet in front of him and scrolled through the latest internal company news—an upcoming presentation, board minutes, notes on regions, etc. This morning he was absentmindedly looking at the monthly store-by-store numbers. The more he read, the faster he scrolled: the numbers unfurled before him like a banner of misery. Lost customers. Lost customers. Lost customers. It was the same everywhere: a mass hemorrhage. Their huge marketing promotion hadn't done squat.

One row caught his eye as he scrolled. It had some green on it. Green was rare. Green was good. It represented progress. He clicked on a button in the corner to go to store details.

"Well, I'll be damned," he said to the empty room. The green was for Zero.

He kept scrolling through as he entered minute seven of his

plank. Every other gym was red. At seven minutes he couldn't scroll and plank anymore. He shut his eyes, funneling all his strength into the mental battle. Finally, at eight minutes and fifteen seconds, Roland dropped. *Damn.* Fifteen seconds short of his max of 8:30.

He rested a moment, toweling off his head and then went to the elliptical, bringing his tablet with him. He went back to the Zero slide. It was interesting, but it didn't tell him enough. Still on the elliptical, Roland called John. He was hoping John was busy and he could just leave him a mess—

"Hey, Roland!"

Oh, well.

"Hey John," Roland said with forced enthusiasm. "I heard things are going well over there."

There was a chuckle on John's end. "Oh, so you saw the numbers?"

"I did."

"And . . ."

Roland slowed the elliptical down to catch his breath and actually talk. "I'm proud of you, bro. It looks like your cost-cutting is really paying off. Just as I knew it would."

"Thanks, Roland. I gotta tell you, we've gotten a lot more curious over the last couple of months. And you can see the results. It's been eye opening, to say the least."

"I'm sure it has. That's what I was hoping would happen when I sent you down there. I always trusted that you'd make an impact at Zero, John. Never doubted it."

"That's the thing, though—it wasn't just me. You got time to talk about it now? I feel like we're on to some pretty big stuff down here."

"I always have time to talk with you, but right now's not the best time to go into specifics. I'm sort of busy at the moment."

There was a pause.

"Roland, I can hear the TVs in the background. You're breathing through your nose like a hog. You're in your gym."

"As I said, I'm busy."

"Humor me, Roland. We've been trying a lot of changes around here. At first, kind of taking stabs in the dark, but I've been actually listening to customers and trainers and we've really hit on some ideas that can be scaled relatively easy."

Roland was partially paying attention to John and partially watching TV. Of course John thought he was on to the next big thing. That was the great thing about John—his enthusiasm. It was back. John was engaged. But that enthusiasm was also a double-edged sword. John often mixed up enthusiasm for good ideas. Roland was trying to figure out how to tell John he didn't need or want any of his "innovative" ideas, he just wanted his enthusiasm. Roland allowed himself to daydream on the elliptical for a second—oh man! If he had a thousand Johns, then he'd be set. That's what this company was missing—passion.

"Mm-hmm," Roland said. "Sounds awesome, brother. But the reason I called was actually to give *you* some big news. You want to hear about something that's going to change GF and all gyms forever?"

"You sound like an infomercial."

"Don't knock infomercials, they move product. Look, John, the traditional gym model is dying. It's getting disrupted by all this new tech, from Peloton to Workout Apps to Orange theory. In its current form, this business is unsustainable. If we have any chance of making it, we have to do something bold. We have to reinvent fitness. John, the reason I've been pushing cost cutting so much is that I needed the funds to buy Reach-3D."

He paused for a reaction but John was quiet. Roland continued on, untroubled. "And here's the best part. I want you to run it!" It was a decision Roland had made just now, but that was an unimportant detail.

He paused again. John didn't seem to understand. All he could muster was a "huh?"

"Reach-3D, John. Reach-3D! You know, the fitness startup. It's been all over the news this year."

John didn't say anything. Roland smiled. He could just imagine John pumping his fists up and down excited on the other end. It felt good to offer this golden opportunity to his brother, to give him another shot at the big-time.

"Never heard of it."

Taken aback, Roland quickly explained. GF had agreed to purchase one of the rising start-up companies in the tech and fitness world. Reach-3D used three-dimensional body-scanning technology, along with artificial intelligence, to tell members in real time if their posture during different exercises was correct. It currently had one hundred different exercises and was adding more all the time. Plus, it had virtual encouragement assistants—customizable cheerleaders. The two aspects worked together. As Roland explained it, he got excited. "This is a game changer, big brother! GF used to be on the cutting edge of innovation in fitness, and Reach-3D going to put us back where we belong."

John's voice was very measured. "That app sounds a lot like what trainers do, Roland."

"You get it! Exactly! GF won't need any more trainers! That overhead is crushing us, John. And you are going to be the one to implement it! Consider it a small reward for turning things around. You helped make this company what it is. Now it's time be a part of the future. You'd be an executive again, with all your old perks back and then some. Come turn this company back into the industry leader it was meant to be."

John exhaled into the phone; the noise was like waves retreating from the shore. "If you'd just let me talk for a minute. We've made all this progress here. I'd really like to tell you about how we're moving the needle."

Roland rolled his eyes. Why didn't John ever *listen*? "John. With all due respect, we need to move a much bigger needle. I need to know right now: are you in?"

CHAPTER TWENTY

"WHAAAAT?!"

Mr. G 's face was a shade of red commonly associated with fire hydrants and strangulation. They were in John's tiny office with the door closed—John had taken precautions—but even so, Mr. G had screamed loud enough that everybody in Zero heard him. Heck, people in the GF fifty miles away probably heard him.

"Replacing trainers with robots is *criminal*! It's goddamned *criminal*!"

John looked wanly at Mr. G. "So, you don't approve?"

"Don't approve?" Mr. G spluttered, waving his hands. "The fact that you are even *considering* participating in something like this is disgraceful. This is not a step into the future. This is a step into the tar pit of bankruptcy and Roland is the wooly mammoth diving in head-first."

"I'm on the same page!" John put up his hands defensively; it looked like Mr. G was about to start swinging. "I agree with you. But think of it this way: this project will put me back at the headquarters where I can really change things."

"What about all the things you've done here?"

"That's exactly why I need to get back to the Mothership.

Now I have the knowledge of how to make an actual difference. I know the importance of getting curious and I can teach them the process for how to do it. I agree it's not the way I saw this playing out, but opportunity doesn't always open the door you are expecting."

"You can't just replace the personal relationship our trainers have with technology, John! I didn't think I had to explain this to you, of all people. You're seriously considering helping Roland just get rid of all the trainers?"

"Look. I've been researching the technology. It's gotten a ton of investment and buzz. And I don't think it means we have to get *rid* of trainers, it could mean giving trainers another tool they can use to help customers reach their goals. And now we know so much more about how to introduce trainers to new tech—"

Mr. G groaned and dragged his fingers down his cheeks, leaving white lines that quickly faded back to red. Some days he wished he'd never opened another location after Zero. He was still working out at Zero—what more did he need? And now, instead of living the fun and carefree life that success was *supposed* to bring him, he was focused on some crap that he could see from a mile away was a disaster. He shook his head. He'd heard enough about this garbage idea.

"Johnny, come with me," Mr. G beckoned. He led him out of the office and over to the weights area. John looked confused as Mr. G started loading weights onto the bench press bar. He was going for a true Cadillac: two forty-five-pound plates on each side of the forty-five-pound Olympic bar. Two hundred twenty-five pounds total. Then he lay down under the bar. Alarmed, John came around to offer him a spot—he had to be impressed with the amount of weight.

Mr. G nodded. John helped him with a liftoff and then stood over him nervously as Mr. G completed five flawless reps and put the bar back without needing any help. John shook his head, dumbfounded.

"That's amazing. What are you, sixty-eight, and you're still banging out Cadillacs?"

"Well, I had you, John, a trainer, helping me. I don't care how smart the phone in my pocket is, it can't give me a spot."

John was quiet.

"And I bet the people who developed this robot or app or whatever this Reach-3D is, they didn't think about that. Because none of them are lifters. None of them are true gym rats." He picked up a towel and wiped down the bench. "You can still do the right thing here, John."

"What do you think that is, though?"

Mr. G started unloading the weight off the bar, saying nothing. Then finally he turned to John and drew himself up to his full height. He wasn't as tall as John, but he was a force to be reckoned with.

"Tell Roland what his board won't. No. N-O. And then quit and don't turn back. Didn't you learn anything from listening to our customers? If someone wants to work out with technology, they can get an app. If they want a specific class like yoga or spinning or boxing or dance, they can go to a place that specializes in that. What our customers are telling us, if you were listening, is how much they valued that trainer relationship."

Mr. G got nose-to-nose with him and poked John's chest. "Mark my words, you want no part in this."

CHAPTER
TWENTY-ONE

EVEN AT NIGHT, WITH ALL ITS NEON BEER SIGNS ABLAZE AND its barstools full, the Pour House was no one's idea of elegance. But in the cold light of day, with the sun coming in gray through the bleared windows and all the cracks visible in the cheap stucco walls, it was like a particularly cynical vision of the afterlife. Yet it was right, John reflected, that he should have wound up here. It was where this entire adventure had begun half a lifetime ago. Or rather two months ago, but it had felt a lot longer. Two tectonic-level shocks to one's professional life will have that effect.

The first month back at GF had been rough—for every step forward it felt like three steps back. Without Mr. G, he wouldn't have even tried. But getting to hang out with Mr. G again had been the morale booster John needed when he was at his lowest. When they worked out together, their years fell away like snakeskin, and they both felt twenty years younger.

But then Mr. G's original hunch about pricing and fees had turned out to be incorrect. GF members didn't care that much about a few dollars here and there as they did about the trainer interactions. Looking back, it made sense—but most things did when you looked back at them. And now, Roland was about selling a new experience and the more research John did into Reach-3D, the more it seemed like it might take off. After all, investors had poured $10 million into the company. By this point, John had learned not to assume he was the only expert—so what did they know that he and Mr. G didn't?

This was a big dilemma that needed an outside perspective, and there was only one outsider John trusted to help him think it through. The problem was that he'd sort of burned a bridge with that outsider when he'd awkwardly attempted to make out with her only to be interrupted by his ex.

So here he was back at the Pour House. It was John's *mea culpa* to Sam. Except she was late. John toyed with the idea of ordering another beer, but he remembered what happened the last time he drank here.

John didn't know if she'd actually show. He had to admit she didn't have a lot of reasons to come. She certainly didn't owe him anything, and he owed her everything. She had gotten nothing out of this deal except some headaches, one moment of pure mortification, and a lot of bullheadedness from John and Mr. G.

John wanted to change that. But to do so, Sam had to make an appearance. He was just about to break down and drink the top-shelf scotch he'd ordered for her, when she walked through the door.

She approached with her signature confident gait. Like she owned the bar—or more like she *could* have owned the bar, if it weren't such a dump. "Long time no see," Sam said, alighting on a barstool.

"I was just about to start drinking this." John held up her scotch.

Sam took it from him and sniffed it. "You remembered. So, you work things out with Kelsey?"

"About as well as I worked them out with you."

Sam laughed at that and took a drink. "Your skills with the ladies are second to none, John."

"I oughta write a book," he moaned.

Sam put her drink down and fixed him with a look. Flirtation done. Business time. "Now tell me what was so important you were willing to risk personal humiliation by bringing me here?"

John explained Reach-3D and the opportunity to Sam, as well as Mr. G's warnings. She asked good questions that John hadn't even thought about. And he started taking notes on the back of a cocktail napkin.

Finally, thirty minutes and a very restrained drink and half later, John finished explaining and venting. He downed the remaining half of his drink and turned to her imploringly.

"So what do I do? I feel like I'm stuck between two experts!"

"You are."

"Mr. G is the rock and Roland the hard place and whether I zig or zag, I'm going to have to make a decision soon."

"How soon?"

John pointed to his watch. "I've got a red-eye to the Mothership in six hours."

Sam whistled low and propped her elbows on the bar. "A battle of two experts. Past versus future. Sounds like a summer blockbuster to me." She ruffled her hair, thinking, then sat upright and brushed her hair back and fixed her eyes on John's. They were less than a foot away from one another.

"So what would you do?" John asked.

"Reach-3D is definitely a disruptive idea. It's the other kind of innovation we didn't really talk about. And as I told you, I think it's important that a company spend most of its efforts on those everyday innovations, the low-hanging fruit, but it's important to also spend some resources—*some*—on the higher-risk, higher-reward moonshots. The problem is **most companies worry about whether they CAN create something new and radical, but they don't spend enough time asking whether they SHOULD create it**. It could be big, but it could also be a dud. I'd try to figure out the riskiest assumptions with this idea and test them in some low-cost, low-effort way. You don't need the actual technology to figure out if customers value the idea."

"So you think it's a good bet?"

"I haven't the faintest idea, John. The problem is neither do Roland or Mr. G. They are both just going off gut instinct. Neither one is very curious. Roland seems to be blinded by the shiny object—he's expecting the projections to carry this company forward, and anyone who has launched a new disruptive idea will tell you the projections go out the window on the first day. And Mr. G, well . . . he's just against it on principle. And maybe because he hates the idea of his company firing so many people."

John moved back and asked, "How do I make them curious?"

"Ha! They are both entrenched in being right. The only thing you can do is be curious yourself. Even in your short timeline."

"This is why I come to you! You know what? You're my Curiosity Muse."

Sam laughed again. "What can I say. You've helped me out too, you know."

"Me?"

"From your place. After that crazy . . . incident that night, I really did a lot of reflecting. You know, I've never applied being curious to my personal life. I've always put up a barrier between business and pleasure. And talking with you made me think all this blind-spot talk also applies to personal relationships. And I've got this old flame in Vegas that I kind of left on bad terms ..."

"No kidding."

"Uh huh. And honestly, doing a little introspection made me realize I hadn't done very much listening. Talk about the pot calling the kettle black."

"So what are you doing about it?"

"Me and the guy are talking. And I'm finally listening. Nothing big, no one's sprinting to the airport and flying across the country, but I feel better about myself."

"Is that why you came today?"

"I don't like to see good people flailing." Sam lowered her voice, and her whole expression softened. "The guy in Las Vegas was a lot like you, John. When I met him, he was at the end of his rope. So close to the finish line, but not able to see it. And just like you, he needed a little nudge. I questioned myself for a while about why I was helping you. It wasn't just because I wanted to get my shoes back. It was because I liked who I was when I was doing it."

This was a side of Sam John hadn't seen before—one he wouldn't have guessed even existed. But now that he was seeing it, he understood that it was the side of her that made all the other things—the savvy, the confidence, the willingness to be wrong—possible.

"I like you, John. I like Mr. G, and I even like Kelsey. And I've found that there are worse weaknesses to have than not being able to say no to good people who need a little help." Sam twirled the straw in her drink. "And I also like the hopefully free drinks."

John gazed at Sam. This time, he didn't hesitate at all. He knew what to do.

He gave her a hug. A big bear hug.

"The drinks," he said, his voice muffled by her shoulder, "are definitely on me."

"Hey," she patted his back, "this isn't goodbye. I'm still a gym member! But I think you've got the idea. You've taken the nudge."

"I have. Thank you, Sam. For everything. And I promise to stay curious."

"I'm warning you, once you start, it can be hard to stop." Sam gathered her things. "Oh—and say hi to Kelsey, will ya?"

"For you?"

"For yourself, John."

CHAPTER
TWENTY-TWO

DAWN WAS JUST BREAKING WHEN JOHN ARRIVED AT THE park. The grass was still wet and the air was chilly, even with his hoodie on. He was still shaking off the stiffness from the late flight in. He jogged at a slow pace, trying to warm up without burning too much energy. He knew the importance of what he was about to do, and jogging always helped him focus when he was anxious.

It was still too dark to see the entire park, but at John's first glance it seemed empty. Crap, he thought, maybe this crazy plan he developed on the plane was for nothing. He focused his eyes and scanned more slowly. There! Near the swing set, he spotted a figure. Not much more than a shadow at this distance, but John would have known that shadow anywhere.

John walked up slowly, feeling the dew-slick grass underneath his Reeboks. His heart was about to jump out of his chest. It was the same feeling as giving a best man speech or going on a first date. As he got closer to the swing set he could see the silhouette stretching with his back to him. John took a deep breath.

"Hey Roland."

Roland almost jumped out of his gym socks. He whirled around, about to yell bloody murder, but when he saw who it was, he froze. Almost too quickly, he regained his composure, as if being snuck up on by his banished brother at a park at dawn was the most normal thing in the world.

"I didn't realize you were coming in today, John."

John spread his arms wide. "Surprise. Was just wondering if you'd done your plank yet."

"Plank? My plank?" Roland looked at John as if trying to figure out whether he'd finally lost it. "Uh, no? I mean I was going to do it. But I'm stretching."

John nodded, enjoying Roland's confusion. "Mind if I do it with you?"

"Since when do you plank?"

"Humor me. I just flew halfway across the country."

Roland snorted. "Sure. Whatever's going on here, sure. You can plank with me. I'm not going to stop when you get tired, though."

"Trash talk already, Rollie?" John reverted to Roland's child nickname. It was his way of letting Roland know he wasn't his CEO, he was his little brother. "No worries. I won't ask you to."

Roland looked at his watch. It was one of those gaudy smartwatches with an unnecessarily big band. "Ready when you are."

John immediately got down on the grass. Arms at right angles, his weight distributed evenly throughout his body. Back straight. Legs spread to shoulder-width apart. Feet rigid. Online videos, his interviews, research—all the fruits of his curiosity—working in harmony.

John looked up at Roland. "You joining?" Roland took a couple of shallow breaths and got down alongside him. The battle was on.

Immediately, John noticed that Roland's elbows were too

far in. Roland was giving himself a weaker base than what was ideal. John also noticed that Roland's breaths remained shallow. He wasn't using his full lung capacity. John, on the other hand, felt great. The crisp morning air was refreshing, and actually taking a break for a couple of days had given his ab muscles time to recover. He was feeling confident enough that he turned to look at Roland.

"Do you know why I'm here?" Roland was looking at the ground. He grunted but didn't respond. John knew he wasn't tired but conserving energy. John thought for a second about doing the same. But no. He had to not only beat Roland, but make his point.

"I'm not here to accept the job. Nor am I here to turn down the job."

"Uh huh." Whatever Roland was thinking, he didn't let on.

There was a long pause. John steadied his shoulders again. His shoulders and his forearms were his weak points, that's what he'd learned. If John kept them strong, he'd hit eight minutes. Or at least he'd have a chance. He concentrated on how pleasant the cool damp grass felt on his forearms.

After a while, Roland glanced up at John and then at his watch. "Two minutes."

John decided to talk again. This was the window he had to make his case; he couldn't waste it. He shifted his weight just a touch, so he could look Roland dead in the eye.

"You were right that Mr. G and I tried some stuff, but you didn't want to hear about it the other day, so I figured I'd catch you up at a time when you had nothing else to do but listen. You were also right that I should be careful about listening to Mr. G. I guess that's why you're in charge of GF and I'm just a store manager."

A long silence. An hour seemed to go by before Roland finally grunted, "Four minutes. Get. To. The. Point." Even in the darkness, John could see Roland sweating. Big drops of sweat fell from his brow and burst on the grass. John shifted his weight yet again. He was starting to feel the strain too.

"The point is that I'm sorry and you were right. It's tough for me to admit but you were right when you sent me to Zero. I wasn't listening to you. I wasn't listening to anyone. I was focused on my own pride and so deep in my own expert mindset—so convinced I knew everything about innovation—that I never paused to consider that perhaps, I didn't." Talking, he found, distracted him from the pain gathering in his shoulder blades.

"Six . . ." Roland huffed, then did some Lamaze-style rapid breathing, then finished: ". . . minutes."

"So you maybe weren't expecting to see me this early in the morning. But, you know, it's always better to apologize in person."

Roland just grunted again. John could feel his forearms and abs straining. It was a battle of will now, not strength. Thirty more excruciating seconds passed in silence. Dawn broke over the two Hunt brothers in a park, fighting their own bodies and each other. They were grown now, but the childhood competitiveness was as strong as it had ever been.

John had started a new mantra of his: "I'm breathing in. I'm breathing out." He knew from practice he could hold his plank until the end of the chant, and renew it with every breath. He repeated in his mind, "Breathing in, I'm calm. Breathing out, I smile."

He kept repeating it. But he was having trouble staying in the moment. He tried to slow the chant down. But then it ended and he started again. He was weakening now, his biceps rubbery and the knives pushing slowly into his stomach. Whatever his mind was trying to tell itself, he was having trouble breathing, and Roland was still going. He'd miscalculated. Panic flared through John's mind. *One more time!* he willed himself. He could not let Roland beat him.

The panic provided a small jolt of energy. Not a lot, but enough that he started doing a mental countdown from fifteen in his head. Just keep up until zero.

12, 11, 10. Keep it. Nine more seconds! Eight more seconds!

And then from beside him there was a noise like the air going out of a beachball, and Roland dropped.

It was over. John had won.

Roland lay flat on his back, his eyes closed, gulping for air. When he finally opened his eyes they bulged in astonishment at what he saw.

"How are you . . . what is happening?"

John was still holding his plank. His world had winnowed down to the feeling of air flowing into his lungs and out again. He was vaguely aware of some kind of pain in his abs, but it seemed distant, almost as if it were happening to someone else. Triumphal adrenaline and endorphins were surging through his body. He'd heard of a runner's high. This must be a planker's high.

"How are you doing this?" Roland gasped.

"It's just a plank, Rollie."

Roland could hardly speak for ragged breathing. "Don't be—*huff*—cute. I have never seen you do a—*huff*—plank before."

John focused.

"Ten minutes!" Roland shrieked as he looked at his watch. "I've never hit ten minutes."

That would do. John finally lowered his knees. Completely in control. His abs were ready to explode but he wasn't about to let Roland know that. He kneeled on the grass, his back straight, and calmly turned to Roland. "That's true. In fact, I don't think I had really done a plank until two months ago. Not too bad, huh?"

"How?"

"Rollie, you know what the planking world record is?"

"Forty minutes?"

"Try again."

"Fifty?"

"Eight hours and one minute. And the people in that range, they're not genetically-blessed freaks or steroid-chewing super-stars. They're people just like you and me. But with one difference."

"What's that?"

"They never allowed their expert mindset to sabotage them from improving and getting better."

"Their huh?" Roland rubbed his temples. "What are you *talking* about?"

"You asked me to get to the point. Well, here it is: the expert mindset is the name for the disease I had two months ago." John took a moment to catch his breath and sat down next to Roland. They were back to being just two brothers. Moreover, Roland seemed to be listening.

"See, when you become familiar with a task or something, you feel like you've got the hang of it. But then you also stop being curious about it. **You stop trying to improve because you start believing that you're an expert**. Think about it. I knew where to find you because you work out here every morning before work. Five days a week. You do the same exercises in the same order. **And you're stuck with the same results**."

"My plank time is better than everyone else I know, John!"

"It *was* better," John said, firmly but without cruelty. He was finally speaking like an elder brother again. "I'm not trying to tease you or show you up. I know you care a lot about this. I'm just saying that **you can't do the same thing you've always done and expect to continuously improve.** And you can't rest on your laurels because someone might come along one day and pass you by. Whenever I found that I was not improving, I didn't just try to grit my way through more planks with what had worked in the past, I did something about it. I tried to get curious about why I was failing to get better. Instead of thinking my planks were good enough and continuing to do what I had been doing, I tried to find my **blind spots.** Those things I wasn't aware of that were keeping me from innovating and growing. And I certainly never tried to rest on my old routine."

"Well, it seems to have worked," Roland said, sulking.

"Thank you, Roland. That means a lot."

"So glad you spent two months of your life to beat me in planks. Thanks for the lecture."

John couldn't believe Roland still thought they were talking about planks. He wasn't listening to him at all. "Jesus, Roland. No. I didn't do it to beat you at your thing. I did it to get you to listen. Because what I'm telling you applies not just to planking but to GF. Galati Fitness has become completely disconnected from its customers. We've fallen into this expert trap that I'm talking about, where we became more worried about being right than whether we were creating actual *value* for customers! That's why the customers have been leaving at a faster and faster rate after signing up."

"John, that's a pretty gross oversimplification of what's happening. We're losing customers because we haven't evolved. That's where Reach-3D fits in."

"I know it feels that way, but that's only because you haven't considered the possibility that you might be wrong. Here's what I learned happens when we start seeing ourselves as experts. **We become overconfident in our skills and we stop looking for blind spots.** It means that we aren't even aware of what we're doing wrong. That's how I beat you, Roland. You've got blind spots in your plank form. I can see them. But you've also got blind spots in how we're interacting with customers."

Roland was silent.

"Another negative of seeing ourselves as the expert is that we aren't focusing on the right things. Because we're confident, our vision narrows and we only see evidence that backs up our preconceived notions. So we ask superficial questions to confirm those notions, rather than asking, 'am I actually creating value?' I know you aren't asking curious questions about your planks because you could have easily figured out how to get much better by now, instead of plateauing. And I know we aren't asking curious questions of our customers, because I've seen the reports you rely on. They tell you everything's going according to plan, and yet we're losing customers at a faster and faster pace."

Roland looked off in the distance and didn't say a word.

"And really what it boils down to is that when we become an expert, we stop being curious about the things we are doing. **We stop experimenting with ways to do it even better, because we *feel* like what we're doing works. We don't ask if we're focused on the *right* things.** And it seems wasteful when we try things that don't work. So we just keep doing what's always worked in the past. But a lot of the time, we end up missing big changes all around us, and meanwhile, someone new, hungry, and curious comes in out of nowhere and yanks the rug out from under our feet. Blockbuster, Kodak, Blackberry, Borders, CompuServe. I could keep going. This is why companies die. They start believing their own BS and they stop being curious about their customers, their employees, and their products."

Roland stood up and started pacing, covering his mouth with his hand. John pushed forward.

"Listen, Rollie, I'm not 'better' at planks than you. I was just a lot more curious than you about how to improve my time and I didn't become overconfident in what I was doing or delude myself into thinking that I had all the answers. I wasn't afraid to try new stuff out and fail. And I failed a *lot*. I had to give myself space to *test* whether things worked. Like, just a week before I came here, I didn't even hit seven minutes. I had been consistently hitting it before, but I tried something new that day with my foot stance and it didn't work. Instead of taking it personally though, I moved on and well . . . you saw the results."

"Mm." Was any of this getting through to him? John didn't know if he was even listening. He'd give it one more try.

"I swear, I'll never do another plank again unless it's to help you improve yours. I'm not betraying you! I came here to do the opposite. To tell you about what I've been able to do with these new ideas. The same method I used to hit ten minutes? Well, I've been applying them all at Zero."

Roland glanced at John warily. "Is that how you dealt with the attrition? Those numbers seemed unreal, John."

He was finally listening. John felt a wave of relief. "I thought you'd never ask. I realized that the only way to actually figure out what was wrong was to find the tension points that were pushing members away. So I asked them. I let them see that I was genuinely curious about what frustrated them about GF. See, I learned that **no matter how happy they are today,**

their expectations will evolve tomorrow. They will have new needs. I learned that there is always low hanging fruit to find the tensions between you and your customers."

"Sounds like a lot of work."

"It was! And frankly a lot of it sucked. I learned that **honest feedback can hurt.** When members told me that the things I thought were important really didn't matter, that stung. It made me feel like a moron. When I realized that many of the programs I had put into place while at the Mothership had inadvertently caused some of the attrition, it felt like a punch to the gut . . ."

"Wait! What?"

"Yes, Roland. I'll take responsibility. We . . . me . . . the management team . . . implemented all these programs and we didn't realize that we were driving apart our members and trainers through the incentive structures. So I checked my expertise and engaged the trainers to help us come up with a solution. They thought up all these crazy experiments, and they were more engaged than what I've seen in a long time. Roland, in one month we increased revenue by nearly $50,000 and reversed the exodus of members."

John whipped out his phone from his pocket and showed Roland the updated numbers. He had an extra week of data to show that they were sustaining the positive results.

There was a long, heavy silence. Roland, ever the diligent CEO, scanned the data carefully. Finally, Roland handed John his phone back. The sun was coming through the trees now.

John continued. "We didn't have any fancy apps like Reach-3D. It was just Kelsey, Mr. G, and me. And okay, this woman named Sam, too. But we figured out that by actually listening, we could make a big impact with everyday innovations. Just replicating what we did at every location would make a huge impact, Roland. **We can seriously move the needle with stuff like this. We just need to be curious enough to see it.**"

Roland looked at John with a serious stare. "So you think Reach-3D is a bad idea?"

"I don't know Roland. It could be a home run. But it could also be a dud. And the thing is, I don't think you or anyone else knows either. That's the liberating thing about this—I don't *have* to know everything! All we need to do is get a lot more curious about it."

"So what would you do?"

"I'd try to figure out the answers to these four questions," John said.

"One, what are the blind spots to this technology? What are the tension points it causes?

"Two, are you focused on the right things? What is the business problem this technology is going to solve and what are nine other ways we can try to solve that problem?

"Three, what can you test? What kinds of experiments can we run to see if the technology is truly a trainer replacement? Or maybe it's a trainer supplement? How can we find the best application by trying multiple things?

"And four, how can we engage others to help solve this problem? We don't have to just look to gyms to see interesting case studies. Lots of different kinds of companies are trying to re-place human assistance with some form of technology. What can we learn from the tax prep industry, or I don't know, those self-serve therapy apps. The point is, lots of different industries are trying to do something comparable, so what can we learn from them?"

Roland rubbed his cheeks, then let out a low whistle. "You've been giving this some thought."

"I've just learned over the last few months what it really meant to be curious, and how much it can propel you to big discoveries. You and the Mothership are going to have to listen to customers and employees and figure out if Reach-3D actually creates value, or if it's just a very shiny and expensive new toy. No business case can tell you that."

Roland had a constipated look on his face. "You know the board is voting on the acquisition of Reach-3D today."

"I didn't know that. But I know that if the decision was up to me, I'd have a lot more questions about how it could benefit GF."

"The board won't ask many questions. They consider it a done deal."

"Is it?" John looked at Roland. This was the do or die moment.

"It's not done until I say it is."

"And what do you think, Rollie?"

Roland stood there, wavering. He looked around the park. Finally, he murmured something, so quietly that John needed to lean in to hear him: "I think I need to get a lot more curious."

CHAPTER
TWENTY-THREE

MR. G WAS PACING BACK AND FORTH AT THE MOTHERSHIP side exit. He noticed a couple of employees smoking and gave them a curt nod. He didn't have any time to engage in pleasantries. She should have been out by now. Where was Kelsey? Had she been fired? Had second thoughts?

This stupid plan! At first, when John explained it, it sounded like one of those just-crazy-enough-to-work ideas, but the more Mr. G thought about it, the more he realized that "try and out-plank Roland to prove my point" was more like the definitely-going-to-fail kind of crazy.

No matter how much Mr. G tried to work out and play golf and keep his mind off John and GF, he hadn't been able to keep it together. He had started calling Kelsey, sharing his anxiety with her. And then two days ago, he finally figured out why he was so uneasy—John was in over his head. There was a reason Roland was CEO rather than John. But with John "too busy" to talk and Mr. G stuck powerless back at Zero, there was nothing he could do.

Or was there?

Mr. G came up with a different plan. A failsafe. In the inevitable scenario that John's plan didn't work, Mr. G would crash the board meeting and plead his case of why Roland was doing a bad job and why this Reach-3D purchase was a terrible idea.

He was wearing a dark hoodie and looking as inconspicuous as a sixty-eight-year-old musclebound man could. Kelsey, who was back working at the Mothership and had the security badge, would let him in through a side door. They'd take the back steps to the fourth floor. Nobody would know he was there. Until he was ready to bust into the meeting.

But where was Kelsey? He swore under his breath. He was optimistic by nature but even he knew this was a long shot. Still, it felt like their only shot. Mr. G loved John like a son. Yet his real son, his real baby, was GF itself. It had been a fool's errand to send anyone but himself. Only he could save GF.

Finally, the side door creaked open. There was Kelsey.

"Where have you been?"

"I'm so sorry, Mr. G—I couldn't get away earlier. We're going to have to hustle."

"Let's get up there."

The two of them bolted up the steps. Despite the decades separating them, he bounded past her.

The stairs were on the other end of the building from the board conference room so once they got to the fourth floor, they had to keep chugging and running all the way to the other side. Finally, they were in front of the double doors to the executive suite and board conference room. Kelsey fumbled for a second to get her access card to open the doors. She got it in her hand and was ready to swipe when Mr. G grabbed her arm.

"Hold on. We need to calm down. Let's take a breath." Kelsey nodded. She breathed in. Before she even breathed out, he snatched the card from her hand and swiped it himself.

"It's show time!"

They barged into the suite, but they were too late. The door at the far end of the room was open and everyone was filing out through the other entrance. Mr. G felt like he'd been punched in the stomach. They had missed their shot.

And then Mr. G felt a tap on his shoulder. He turned around only to be wrapped in a hug from a very burly man. Mr. G couldn't believe it.

"John! You're alive!"

"Never better!" Grinned John. He released Mr. G and went to hug Kelsey too, but she backed up. He settled for giving her a simple pat on the shoulder.

Mr. G looked at John, "So what's the verdict?"

Suddenly Roland walked in. "The verdict is this. Turns out my older bro here is not only pretty good at planks, but not as dumb about business as he looks."

"Roland and I talked," John said. "I listened to him and he listened to me. It made for a very nice change."

"Annnd? Get to the point!" Mr. G was chomping at the bit.

John smiled. "GF is in good hands. We worked some stuff out. I'm no longer manager of Zero and I'm back at the Mothership, but I'm also not in charge of Reach-3D. Nobody is."

"So they didn't buy it! I won!"

"Actually, they did buy it. Or rather, invested in a portion of it."

"Oh." Mr. G's face fell.

"But!" Roland stepped in, "John had an interesting idea. A very interesting idea. How would you be interested in helping with Reach-3D, Mr. G? If you're interested, you can help shape the future of fitness. Not by trying to replace trainers, but by making the full experience better. You can help figure out how we can use this tool to scale what trainers are able to do for clients, to be their eyes and ears in a lot more places than they can physically go."

For maybe the first time in his life, Mr. G was entirely tongue-tied.

He wasn't sure he wanted to be associated with this project, but he certainly wouldn't want anyone but him in charge of something that could impact the lives of his trainers in such significant ways. And who was he kidding? Retirement was boring. Fishing and golfing . . . they got old fast. The last few months had made it clear that what he really wanted was to be involved with GF again. This could be the opportunity to spearhead the evolution of his gym. The idea got him fired up.

"I'll do it under one condition," he said, warily. "You guys have to be ready to admit that this fancy-shmancy tech stuff doesn't work. That the gyms might be better off without it."

"That's the whole point," said Roland. "I *don't* know if it'll work or not. I'm genuinely curious. I'm asking if you can be too. That's all I'm asking. That you go in curious."

"Yeah," said Mr. G. slowly. "I can do that. I feel like I got my ass kicked these last few months trying to be right all the time, and I got the message loud and clear: we're going to get a lot further by having the right questions than having the right answers."

"Yes!" John exulted, pumping his fists. "That's exactly it!"

"Plus," Roland winked, "I guarantee you'll never need a badge to get into the building again."

Mr. G's eyes went wide. "What's there to think about? I'm in!"

That got a big laugh.

"Wait, so what are you going to be doing, John?" Mr. G was

curious. He had really missed working with John over the last few years.

"We're actually forming a new insights team!" John exclaimed. "Not just customer insights but company-wide, that will include both customers and the employees. I'll be like the chief listening officer."

"Or the Chief Curiosity Officer." Roland chimed in. He clapped John on the back. The two of them really seemed to be getting along.

"So great." It was Kelsey. She'd sort of shrunk to the corner of the room. She was smiling but Mr. G could see the smile was just a formality. She looked shell-shocked. John went over to her.

"I had two things to tell you, Kelsey. The first thing is that data management is not going anywhere. Isn't that right, Roland?" Roland nodded. "It's an integral part of this operation. Your data is going to help us make much faster decisions on what's working and what's not, so that we can stop wasting resources on things that aren't really helping the business. I showed Roland how indispensable you have been to the team and . . ." he glanced at Roland.

"We'd like to make you the Director of Insights and Analytics at GF, effective immediately. New office on the fourth floor, a big pay bump and some extra vacation days, so that hopefully, the next time you try to save the company from itself, you won't have to sacrifice any important trips to do so."

Kelsey looked at Roland with something very much like wonder in her eyes. And then she paused, mentally shifted gears and asked, "How long do I have to think about it?"

"What's there to think about?" John erupted.

"Don't get me wrong, I love GF and this sounds like a great opportunity, I just have a lot of questions."

"Take some time," Roland reassured her. "This is a lot to process in short order. Why don't we schedule some time to go over your questions?"

Kelsey thanked Roland, turned to John and thrust out her jaw. "And the second thing?" she asked sharply.

John took a step closer to her. "The second thing is I'd like to take you to dinner tonight, Kelsey, if you'll let me. I've been doing a lot of thinking and there's a lot I didn't say that I should have said. Nothing really happened with me and Sam. It almost did, but I actually spent the whole time talking about you."

Kelsey's smile dropped, and she crossed her arms, her face darkening as John continued. "I took us for granted. I took you for granted. You know, one of the biggest things I learned in the last few months is that **what really turns someone into an expert is familiarity. The more comfortable you get with something, the less curious you become.** I had all these reasons for wanting to break up, but the more I thought about it, the more I realized that it was me. I stopped being curious about you . . . about us. I want you to go to dinner with me. I want to ask you a million questions. I feel like I have so much catching up to do."

Kelsey's arms stayed folded, and she tried to keep her expression stern. But try as she might, she couldn't keep her lower lip from quivering. "John Hunt . . . are you asking me out?"

He grabbed her by the shoulders. "That's exactly what I'm doing."

She backed away from his hands, staring at the floor. But when she came up, she came up smiling. It was the first genuine smile Mr. G had seen her give in months.

"I'm listening."

CHAPTER
TWENTY-FOUR

RANDY SLOWLY UNLOCKED THE DOOR. HE'D BEEN ON opening shift at the gym many a groggy morning, but this brisk cold sunrise was different—he was opening up Galati Fitness Zero for the first time as general manager.

As he entered the gym, he slowly twirled the keys in his hand, taking in the moment. All the lights were off. He savored the sound of the keys—his keys—jingling in the silence. In less than twenty minutes, the first members would begin arriving, and the clank of weights would begin, even though the gym didn't technically open for forty more minutes. They had some early birds and Randy wanted to keep ensuring they felt welcome.

He went to the back of Zero and flipped the bank of switches to turn the lights on. Then he went to the cardio machines and flipped the far right elliptical on—that was for Mr. Parson. One of the earliest birds. He had once been a competitive skier, ages ago, but a series of knee operations and age had restricted his workouts. Recently though, he'd become an afternoon bird too. After talking with fellow members, Mr. Parson decided to start using a trainer. It was only a couple of weeks in, but he was already telling Randy about how much stronger his legs felt now that the trainer was incorporating light lower body weights, which avoided hurting his knees, into his workouts. Plus, he winked, he'd been staying away from women. They weakened the knees, he said. Randy smiled to himself. Mr. Parson was a character. The members who were characters were the best.

Randy opened the door to the manager's office. He hadn't been in there in a couple of weeks but was unsurprised to see it nearly bare. John had preferred to be on the floor with the members, not in an office, and Randy felt the same way.

An envelope had been left on the otherwise empty and outdated desk. He picked it up. It was addressed to him. There was a letter inside.

Dear Randy.

Glad to see the manager job went to the best guy I know, and also the guy with the worst taste in booze. You'll do great and you'll be motivated at first. I have no doubt of that. But six months, a year, or even six years down the line, things will get tougher. The days will start to blend together. One day, you may even say to yourself that you've got this manager thing down, that you can run it all on autopilot. You might even feel like an expert at it.

And right then, that's where you have to catch yourself. I tell you this from experience because I let success go to my head. I stopped being curious, stopped listening, and stopped trying to get better. I thought I had all the answers and it took me a while to figure out that I was just fooling myself. To admit that I had actually plateaued. Falling into the expert trap nearly cost me my job and it nearly destroyed the entire GF organization.

quo. You know that there's a big difference between doing your job and creating value. And you think that there are a lot of things your organization needs to be doing to stay competitive.

We want to let you know that you're on the right track and you are not alone. Here's to feeding the fire of curiosity that burns inside you. And here's to using the tools in this book to start the transformation.

About the Authors

ANDY FROMM

Andy is chairman and CEO of Service Management Group (SMG)—a leading, global CX and employee measurement firm that combines technology and insights for the world's leading brands, including a host of Fortune 500 companies. SMG evaluates 250 million surveys across 130 countries annually, helping brands listen better, act faster, and outperform the competition.

Andy founded SMG in 1991 with Bill Fromm and Dr. Len Schlesinger to help brands increase profitable sales by driving employee engagement and customer loyalty. This concept was first articulated in 1998 in *The Service Profit Chain* by Harvard Business School Professors Heskett, Sasser, and Schlesinger.

Andy has served as an expert contributor in the areas of customer experience, employee engagement, and brand research to media such as *The Wall Street Journal*, *USA Today*, and *Fast Company*.

DIANA KANDER

Diana Kander is the *New York Times* bestselling author of *All In Startup*, a novel outlining lessons for launching successful products through the story of a struggling entrepreneur competing in the World Series of Poker.

Diana and her family escaped from the Soviet Union when she was eight years old. By the time she was an American citizen, she had perfected her skills as an entrepreneur—selling flea market goods to grade school classmates at a markup. Diana is a serial entrepreneur and former professor of entrepreneurship in the MBA program at the University of Missouri.

Today, Diana is the director of innovation culture and habits for Maddock Douglas, a Chicago-based innovation consulting firm. In this role, she trains executives and Fortune 1000 companies to be more innovative and to inspire employees to think more like entrepreneurs.

Diana lives in Kansas City, Missouri, with her high school sweetheart and husband, Jason, and their awesome son, True. Fun fact: As research for this book, Diana did an 11.5-minute plank and tore her oblique muscle.

CPSIA information can be obtained
at www.ICGtesting.com
Printed in the USA
BVHW03*0924210918
528171BV00005B/23/P